~

Stuart Robertson's Tips

on

Container Gardening

~

ALSO IN THE SERIES

Stuart Robertson's Tips on Organic Gardening

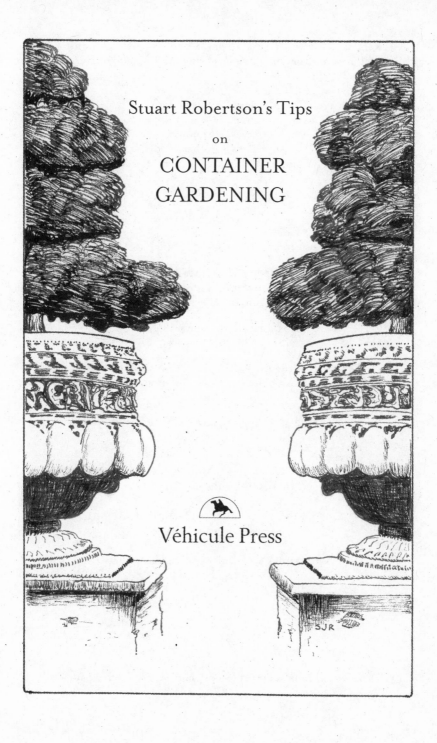

Stuart Robertson's Tips

on

CONTAINER
GARDENING

Véhicule Press

Published with the assistance of the Book Publishing Industry
Development Program of the Department of Canadian Heritage.

Cover designed by David LeBlanc
Cover photograph by Stuart Robertston
Set in Mrs Eaves by Simon Garamond
All drawings by the author
Printed by Marquis Book Printing Inc.

LIBRARY AND ARCHIVES CANADA CATALOGUING IN PUBLICATION

Robertson, Stuart, 1944-
Stuart Robertson's tips on container gardening /
Stuart Robertson

(Stuart Robertson's tips)
ISBN 978-1-55065-240-6

1. Container gardening—Canada. 2. Container gardening—
Snowbelt States. I. Title. II. Series: Robertson, Stuart, 1944-
Stuart Robertson's tips.

SB4i8.R62 2008   635'.9'860971   C2007-907368-9

Published by Véhicule Press, Montréal, Québec, Canada
www.vehiculepress.com

Distribution in Canada by LitDistCo
orders@litdistco.ca

Distribution in U.S. by Independent Publishers Group
www.ipgbook.com

Printed in Canada on 100% post-consumer recycled paper.

To
Donna
who produces the greatest
container gardens

Acknowledgements

This is the second book in a series that I hope will end up stretching across a shelf of your library.

When I published my first gardening book, I felt that it showed a lot of faith on the part of the publisher to encourage me to do it. But it takes even more faith to support the idea of a series of books, particularly when the second book was committed to before the first one was even on the shelves! So I'd like to thank Simon Dardick of Véhicule Press for having so much faith in me, and always being there with kind words and cups of tea.

I've dedicated this book to my wife, Donna Banks, because she really takes over the gardening when it comes to containers. I just do the mixing and heavy lifting. It's her impeccable taste and sense of colour that sets the ever-changing trends for what gets planted in the many and various containers that we own, both in the city and in the country. A lot of the details in Chapter Four about planting arrangements and combinations came from her fertile imagination. Thank you for that, and also for all the cups of tea.

And I would also like to acknowledge all of those fine people who plant up containers and hang them or place them in front of their homes for the rest of the world to appreciate. Walking and driving around various locations during the summer always exposes me to a wonderful deluge of ideas. I see all sorts of things grown in a fascinating array of containers, from zucchini growing in old tires to topiary boxwood shrubs in Grecian urns. And like so many gardeners, the ones who do a lot of their gardening in containers love to talk about it "over the fence". I've had many interesting conversations centered around a planter and a cup of tea.

What is it with me and cups of tea? Perhaps it's my British roots, but it doesn't matter to me if it's orange pekoe, lapsang souchong, black gunpowder or mint. They all fuel my brain and my body in a way that coffee will never do. A cup of tea held in hands that are dirty from gardening is where it's at for me.

Contents

Introduction

Nearly every gardener grows something in a container. It's often a person's first introduction to growing plants either to look at or to eat.

Even if you've got a perfectly good garden to plant flowers and vegetables in, I'll bet you've got at least one pot, window box or planter somewhere.

And for anyone who wants to grow things but who doesn't have a garden, whether they have a third-floor balcony or a back deck, the only alternative is to do it in some sort of container.

So any gardener worth their salt has to know something about growing things in containers. And if you're going to do it, you may as well do it as successfully as possible.

Containers can provide spectacular decorative displays and be a source of goodies for the kitchen. They can also be a bit of a headache. It all depends on how you get started and how you approach the subject. Many of the same principles that apply to gardening at ground level also apply when gardening in containers. But there are also a few differences, and a special set of techniques needs to be learned if you want to get the best from your container gardening efforts.

As in my previous book, *Stuart Robertson's Tips on Organic Gardening*, I'm always looking for ways to reduce the workload for the gardener, and this applies to container gardening as well. And I'm also hoping to attract you to the organic side of gardening, so that your impact on the environment will be as gentle as possible.

Container gardening is an up-close and personal type of gardening, where you can really see and feel the results. I've seen containers that have been given names like a pet, where they've been coddled and fussed over more than a new child. And I've seen containers that have given a whole new lease on life to people who thought they might never garden again.

To paraphrase a well-known line from *The Wind in the Willows*, there's really nothing half so much worth doing as messing about in containers.

CHAPTER ONE

The Container

What makes a good container?

Almost anything can be made into a container in which to grow plants. The main criteria are that it holds soil, allows for drainage and won't blow over in the wind. Other than that, you can grow just about anything you like *in* just about anything.

Once you stray from the more traditional types of pots and planters, you can let your imagination be your guide. All types of vessels and constructs can be turned into a place to grow things.

I've seen people grow marigolds in an old boot and tomatoes in buckets. Wheelbarrows and old tires can be seen all over the countryside with plants poking out of them. Containers run the gamut from sophisticated Grecian urns to rustic barrels and boxes.

However, there are certain specifications that any container **must** meet if it's to be a success.

The essential specifications

1. *A container must be able to hold damp soil over at least the course of one growing season.*

This disallows using old cardboard boxes or paper bags as a container, but it does leave a lot of room for your imagination. Just keep in mind that the larger the container, the fewer the problems of drying out and stunted growth.

Your container must be strong enough to hold the weight of its load of wet soil. Most objects that are made for the purpose of growing are rigid enough for this, but it's when you use other less suitable things as containers that you've got to be careful. When dealing with flexible materials such as wood, plastic or metal, make sure there's enough bracing inside or out to hold the sides from sagging outwards under this weight.

Containers mounted on walls or hung off balcony railings **must** be secure enough to hold the weight of the container, the plants and all the wet soil inside. If you're in doubt about the strength of a nail or screw, don't take the risk. Have it looked at by someone with experience, or get some advice on replacing it. There are fasteners for brick, masonry or wood that are made to hold specific weights, and which should not be exceeded.

2. *A container must allow for good drainage of water, whether it comes from the sky or from a watering can.*

Your container should have at least one drain hole in the bottom, about 2.5 cm (one inch) wide. If the container is wider than 60 cm (24 inches) it should have more than one hole. If it's a long window box I'd advise having drain holes every 30 cm (12 inches) along its length.

These drain holes should be as open as possible to allow for a free flow of water. Sometimes they can become blocked by root growth, so you should check for that late in the season. If you want to avoid losing a lot of soil out of a drain hole, you can cover it with a section of old window screen or a piece of pantyhose. Don't cover it with a bit of terracotta pot as this can end up blocking the hole completely. [Fig 1]

There are lots of nice-looking objects that would make great planters, but if they don't have a drain hole to let out excess water, they're useless. In fact they're dangerous for the plants because if excess water builds-up and floods the soil, your plants will suffer from root rot and other growth problems.

If you have a non-draining container you want to use, consider putting a more utilitarian container that's a bit

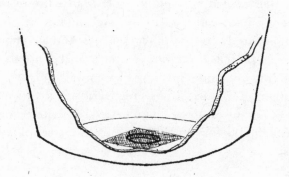

[FIG. 1] SCREEN COVERING DRAIN HOLE

[FIG. 2] CACHE-POT

smaller, like an ordinary plastic pot, **inside** the decorative container. This is called a "cache-pot" or hidden pot. The smaller pot can drain into the larger one, and as long as you check the larger one from time to time to make sure the water isn't building up inside, it will work very well. [Fig 2]

Another alternative, if it's practical, is to drill your own drain holes in the bottom of your sealed container. There are drill bits available for porcelain and masonry as well as metal and plastic.

3. *A container should be as deep as possible, to allow for as much soil as possible to be available to the plants.*

It really doesn't matter how long or how wide your container is, because that just affects how many plants you can cram into it. But what's really important is its depth.

The depth of a container determines just how much soil it can hold, and this in turn determines how much water it will hold. That's the critical point, because it's always going to be the water capacity of your container that will determine how well your plants grow and how much time you have to spend looking after them.

Any basic container, be it a window box or pot, should be at least 20 cm (eight inches) deep. If you look around stores that sell these things, you'll see that there are still plenty of them for sale that are shallower, and their performance (or lack of it) is what gives containers a bad name.

By sticking to this minimum depth of soil, you will allow for good root growth with less crowding and competition for water. It will also act as a deep sponge that holds water much longer in the heat of summer.

The depth of the soil also determines how long the nutrients will last in a container. There are always limited amounts of soil and nutrients in a container, so more soil means more nutrients. And next to water, the nutrients are the most important element in plant growth and performance.

4. *A container should be large enough or heavy enough to stay upright even in a strong wind.*

This may sound such an obvious thing, but I've known lots of cases where pots have been blown over during a summer storm. The last thing you want is to see is your container and plants smashed on the ground after being launched off its perch. It's not only disheartening, it can also be dangerous.

Size

As mentioned in the essential specifications previously, the size of a container will relate directly to how well things grow in it. But the most critical aspect of the size is the *depth*.

You can have a container that's as narrow or as long as you like, but the really critical measurement of its volume will be the depth. The deeper the container, the more soil it can hold, and this is the most important feature of a container.

Containers can only hold a certain amount of soil, and it's this soil that acts as the reservoir of water and nutrients for the plants in the container. As the plants grow their root systems through the season, they are competing for this limited amount of moisture and food. How well the roots grow will determine how well the plants above do. We can keep adding water and nutrients to the soil, but that defeats our attempt to keep the workload to a minimum.

The width and length of a container will determine how many plants you can plant into it, which in turn will affect the amount of moisture and nutrients the plants need as they grow. But no matter what surface area your container has, it's the depth that will determine how often it has to be looked after.

I would recommend that any container be a *minimum* of 20cm (eight inches) deep. If you can provide more depth, that's even better. Unfortunately there are still some containers for sale, particularly window boxes, which are far too shallow to be practical. I've used some homemade window boxes for several years now that are made from 25cm (ten inch) boards.

They have never dried out on me between weekly waterings, even when they're stuffed full of plants and subjected to the driest weather. I can feel how full of moisture they are just by attempting to lift one end of them.

Small containers will dry out much faster than larger ones, for obvious reasons. The soil reservoir is smaller to start with, so there's less moisture available in the first place. Then, depending on how many plants are in it, there will be a constant demand by the roots to suck up moisture to replace what's being lost due to the plant's needs and to evaporation from the plant's leaves. On very hot days, this evapotranspiration rate will be very high, and may exceed the plant's ability to replace the moisture from the planting mixture fast enough, which will cause the foliage to wilt. Some small containers may end up needing to be watered twice a day in the very hottest parts of the summer, which raises your workload and the risks of damage.

Rather that setting up a lot of plants in small containers, which will involve a lot of work keeping them watered, I'd advise putting several plants into one larger container. Along with cutting down on your workload, you'll also be reducing the risk of pots drying out beyond the danger point. I'd recommend using pots no smaller than 20cm (eight inches) in diameter, which gives you about the same depth. This is enough to hold a large geranium or several smaller plants, but it gives you a decent amount of soil.

By having as deep a container as possible, you're increasing the volume of soil that's available to the plants, and thereby reducing the need for frequent feedings and waterings. For example with a container that's 30cm (12 inches) square, for every 2.5cm (one inch) of depth you add, you're adding 2.3 litres (half a gallon) of extra soil, with all its water-holding potential.

Shape

The shape of a container is almost immaterial to its function, with a couple of possible exceptions (always the exceptions!).

A container should not be much narrower at it's base than at it's top. This sort of shape restricts the amount of room for root growth, as well as reducing the amount of soil available as a reservoir. Unless this type of container is very deep, I would avoid using this particular configuration. [Fig 3]

The other container shape to be careful of is one with a neck that's much narrower than the rest of it. This doesn't reduce root growth, but it does make planting and removal rather difficult. It also reduces the potential for air flow into the root area, and you may notice slightly restricted growth as a result. [Fig 4]

There are structural situations to be careful of, particularly with shapes such as long window boxes made out of sections of wood, plastic or metal. If they are longer than 60cm (2 feet), then the weight of wet soil may start to push the sides out of shape unless they are designed with internal bracing. For long boxes I would recommend adding internal or external bracing every 45cm (18 inches). [Fig 5]

Long window boxes also put a lot of force on the fastenings, so they should be very securely mounted.

The same applies to the bottoms of large boxes that are hanging off a wall or railing. If the supports are underneath, this is the safest way. But if the box is attached only along its sides, then there's a lot of pressure on the bottom. In this case either the fastenings must be very secure (screws are best), or there must be added support to hold the bottom in place under any amount of weight. [Fig 6]

What it's made from

What a container is made out of can play an important role in the way it works. There are many materials that are suitable for containers, and few which are less so. Let's start with those that are perhaps less suitable, for one reason or another.

Ironically, one of the most popular container materials is also one of the least suitable. Terracotta or baked unglazed clay has been a traditional material for containers for centuries, but for our busy lifestyles it's probably one of the worst. By its very nature, terracotta is porous so it allows moisture to wick out of it quite quickly. With wind acting upon the surface, the moisture is sucked out at a very high rate, requiring constant attention to keep the soil within moist.

It was this wicking action that made it popular in ancient times. Roots were attracted to the outer edges of the soil ball, as they followed the moisture outwards. This was fine when estates had plenty of gardeners to look after the frequent watering needs of all the potted plants. But these days, we have neither the time nor the staff to look after a lot of needy plants, so terracotta has become a bit of a liability. It still remains one of the moist attractive materials for containers, both large and small, and in order to get around the drying action of the clay, some waterproofing is needed. (See the section later in this Chapter on "Waterproofing").

Metal is a less frequently used material for containers, but it is growing in popularity with its ability to fit into a contemporary styling. In order to resists deterioration due to rusting, the metal should be stainless steel, galvanized or heavily painted. Cast-iron containers are equally prone to rusting, and should also be painted inside and out for their protection.

The main drawback to metal containers is their sensitivity to heat. Under the direct rays of the sun they heat up quite quickly, particularly if they are of a dark colour which absorbs heat more easily than a light one. By heating up they can dry out the soil that is next to the metal, and may even cause damage to roots touching the hot metal.

Containers that rely on basket or woven materials are also a bit of a long-term problem. This material loses its structural integrity when it become very damp, and it also rots quite quickly if it stays wet all the time. Unless your basket container

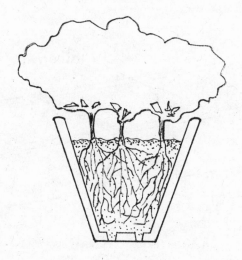

[FIG. 3] POT WITH NARROW BASE

[FIG. 4] POT WITH NARROW NECK

21

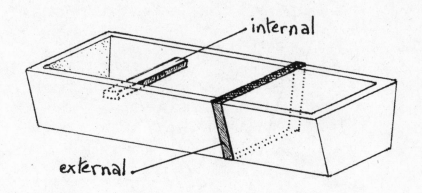

[FIG. 5] INTERNAL-EXTERNAL BRACING

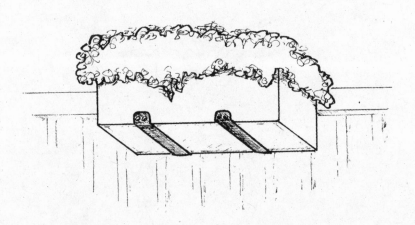

[FIG. 6] SUPPORTING THE BOTTOM

is made from very thick saplings (or wattles), I would suggest using them only for decorative purposes. There should be a plastic liner or a "cache-pot" hidden inside the basket to take the weight and dampness of the soil.

Wood as a container material is another tried-and-tested alternative, but one which also must be selected with care and treated with respect. The only naturally "moisture-proof" woods that are available these days are cedar and redwood. Without any artificial treating of any kind, these woods can withstand moisture almost indefinitely, so they make great materials for plant containers. Wet soil and rainy weather don't affect them at all, and they are an attractive material from which to make containers.

Their only drawback is availability and cost. In many regions it's getting harder to find supplies of finished redwood and cedar from which to make containers, and the cost of the wood is becoming disproportionately high.

You can use many other soft or hard woods for plant containers but they will need to be treated with a preservative to protect them against decaying from moisture. (These treatments are dealt with later in this Chapter under "Waterproofing").

Other than the caveats mentioned previously, almost any other material is suitable for use as a container.

The traditional green plastic pots are still a popular alternative to clay, since they trap moisture in them very effectively. And as mentioned previously, they can be used as cache-pots inside a more decorative container.

Cement and slurries of artificial stone can be cast into many container shapes in molds, and they have the benefit of looking and feeling like the "real thing". They are heavy, even when empty, so they must be originally located with care so that you don't have to move them often.

There are also several synthetic materials finding uses as plant containers.

Foamed-plastic can be manufactured into almost any shape, with all sorts of colours and textures available that mimic other more traditional materials like metal or clay. There are lightweight synthetic containers on sale which, at a slight distance, have all the appearances of old terracotta pots, but because they are plastic they don't have the drawbacks mentioned before.

Fiberglass is very light in weight, and is also being used to form decorative containers in all sorts of shapes and sizes. When painted, it too can take on the aspect of metal and other materials.

Recycled plastics are being used to make planters and window boxes, in a variety of colours. The end product is rather dense and heavy, but the material is nearly indestructible and may be suitable for areas of high traffic or abuse.

Waterproofing

As mentioned before, the big drawback to terracotta is the fact that it's not waterproof, and that water evaporates out of it very easily. To be able to use terracotta pots, but at the same time to overcome this problem, you have a couple of alternatives.

The simplest way of waterproofing an unglazed clay pot, large or small, is to give it a plastic liner before you fill it with any planting mix. Any heavy-duty plastic sheet, such as clear plastic film or cut-up black garbage bags, can be used to line the sides of the pot. Cut a piece that will wrap around the inside of the container from the bottom to just below the top, and then add in some planting mix to hold it in place. Or, you can drop a plastic shopping bag inside the pot, cut a hole in the bottom to let the water out, and then fill it with planting mix. If the plastic is too tall, you can always trim off the excess once the pot is full. [Fig 7]

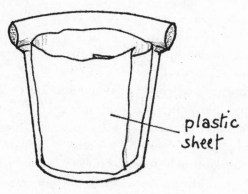

[FIG. 7] PLASTIC LINER

A more permanent way of waterproofing terracotta is to coat it with a waterproofing material. You can use any of the liquids sold to waterproof wood, as once these have dried they don't give off any toxic fumes and won't break down under moist conditions.

You should definitely coat the inside of the container to hold the moisture. You can do the outside as well, but this may give the terracotta a shiny look which you don't want. Test a section on the bottom of the container first, to see if you like the coated look. If not, coating the inside is sufficient to stop the moisture from evaporating.

Wood preservatives can also be used to protect wooden containers, both on the inside and the outside. Untreated wood will absorb moisture over time, particularly from the inside, and this will lead to rotting and a breakdown of the wood. Two coats of a wood preservative are recommended for the inside of a container, while one coat usually suffices for the outside.

As mentioned before, the only readily available untreated woods that resist this rotting action are redwood and cedar.

Of course, you can always paint an untreated-wood container with two coats of coloured paint or wood stain to protect it from the elements. But you'll have to paint the *inside* first with wood preservative to stop the moisture seeping in to the wood. These coats will have to be re-applied periodically, and you must wait for the wood to dry **completely** before re-applying or the liquid will not adhere properly and will peel off quite soon after.

Using treated wood for plant containers avoids this problem altogether. Although treated wood can be painted or stained for decorative purposes, there is no need to do this for protective reasons. The wood has been pressure-treated to force a waterproof wood preservative into the outer layer of the wood. The deeper the pressure-treating, the more expensive the wood will be.

Older versions of this type of preservative used to be quite toxic to plants, as it evaporated off the wood and could contaminate the soil and roots inside. The newer versions of wood preservative are less volatile, and don't have any adverse effect on plants. However, you should always take precautions not to breathe the dust when working with pressure-treated wood, as it can be toxic if inhaled. And **never burn** pressure-treated wood, as the smoke is very toxic to mammals.

Heat proofing

Metal containers don't usually need to be made waterproof, but if they do you can coat the inside area with pitch or fill any cracks with putty. To protect raw metal from rust, use a clear metal preservative or an oil-based paint made specifically for rust proofing. But be warned; if you scratch this preservative or paint when mixing soil or planting, you are exposing the metal to corrosion once again.

Metal containers can heat up quite quickly if exposed directly to the sun, particularly if they are a dark colour that absorbs the heat. The heat can dry out your planting mixture and even burn the roots of plants that touch the metal. To avoid both of these problems, you can line inside of the exposed faces with thin sheets of foamed plastic insulation to keep the metal out of contact with the planting mixture. [Fig 8]

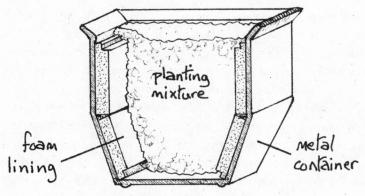

foam lining

planting mixture

metal container

[FIG. 8] HEAT-PROOF INSULATION

Winter-proofing

The materials that your containers are made from will determine how well they get through the winter.

Porous materials such as terracotta, cement and certain stone slurries will gradually absorb water over the growing season. If they are left outdoors and exposed to freezing temperatures during the winter, this moisture inside the porous material will expand and soon crack or shatter it. The best protective measure is to empty the container of planting mixture (to make it lighter), and bring it into a location where it can gradually dry out and where it won't freeze during the winter.

Containers made of unpainted or unpreserved wood will also tend to absorb moisture, but they are more flexible and seem to be able to withstand the freezing action of the winter outdoors more easily.

Metal and all the modern plastics are almost impervious to the action of the winter, so they need very little extra protection.

The only action that might affect a container during the winter is if it's left outdoors full of planting mixture. When moist it will expand as it freezes, and this expansion can exert quite strong pressures on any material. So my recommendation is to partially empty the planting mixture from all of your containers in the autumn when you remove the plants.

I'm suggesting only "partially" removing the soil mix for two reasons. The first is because as long as the container is only half full, the moist mixture won't expand too much or do much damage. And secondly, for purely pecuniary reasons, why get rid of all the soil each season and then have to replace all of it next spring. By only removing half of it (into the compost pile) you can mix it up with some fresh additions next spring at a much lower cost. I can't help it; it's the Scot in me.

For details on keeping certain plants in containers safely during the winter, refer to the section on "Over-wintering plants outdoors" in Chapter Six.

Basic Container Designs

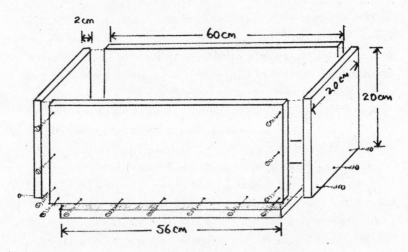

[FIG. 8] BASIC SMALL WINDOW BOX

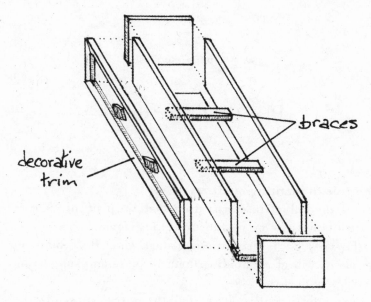

braces

decorative trim

[FIG. 9] BASIC LONG WINDOW BOX

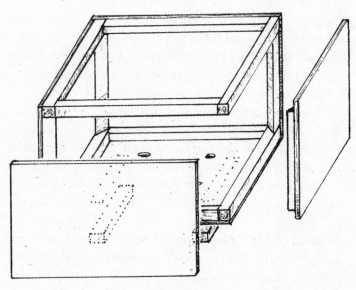

[FIG. 10] BASIC PLANTER

CHAPTER TWO

Planting Mixtures

The role of planting mixtures

As with the soil mixture in a garden bed, the planting mixture in a container has several functions to perform.

First of all, it is the medium through which the roots of all the plants will grow, holding them in place and supporting their upper growth.

Secondly, it is the source of all the nutrients used by the plant to build its parts and grow over the length of a season.

And finally, but most importantly, it is the reservoir for the moisture needed by the plant to stay healthy.

Along with these main structural functions, the planting mixture in a container also has to encourage certain chemical activity, just like garden soil does. It's this chemical activity that turns various inorganic and organic sources of nutrients into a form that is ingestible by the roots of the plant.

As water passes through the mix, it breaks down the various materials into what is called the "soil solution". This is a soup of molecules that contains the nutrients in a form that can be absorbed by the roots of the plant. Having the correct blend of ingredients in the planting mix is the only way to ensure that the soil solution has all the correct nutrients available for the plants.

The passage of water being pulled down by gravity through the planting mix also plays another very important role in plant health. As the water drains downwards, it pulls air in behind it. When you pour water into a small pot, as it drains downwards you can actually hear the air being sucked into the planting mixture. This air provides the plant roots with a majority of the carbon used by plants in their growth, as well as some oxygen, hydrogen and nitrogen. So the actual structure of the planting mixture has to encourage proper water flow if this gas exchange is to take place. [Fig 11])

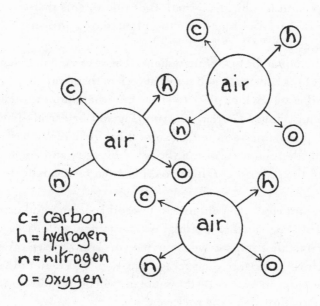

c = carbon
h = hydrogen
n = nitrogen
o = oxygen

[FIG. 11] AIR EXCHANGE

No matter what type of container you're using, or what collection of plants you're growing in it, the planting mixture in the container is therefore the key to how things will grow.

This mixture is the sponge holding the moisture for the plants, and it also contains the nutrients needed by the plants. It's these two factors of moisture and nutrients which will control how well the plants perform at all times, *and they are the two factors that will concern us the most in any type of container growing.*

Ingredients

Since a container holds only a certain amount of material, it's really important that the growing medium you use be the best possible mixture for the job.

I use the word "mixture", because it's usually best to have a variety of ingredients making up your planting mixture. Each of the ingredients will bring certain attributes and assets to the mix, and it's this combination of ingredients that should add up to an ideal blend for the plants being grown in the container.

Let's look at the type of ingredients that we can use in a planting mix for a container, and see what each of them can do for us.

Soil is an obvious place to start, but what kind of soil are we talking about? Garden soil, potting soil or earth? These are all just names applied to something that really has no carefully defined description. So we should try and agree, at least for the purposes of this book, just what we mean by these terms.

When it comes to containers, the soil I recommend using should be a high quality "potting" or "container" soil, packaged by a reputable company whose name you know or see often. The actual material in the package may even be a blend of soil and compost, in which case the company will be proudly stating this on the outside of the package.

Packaged potting soils differ from the soil taken from your garden in many ways, but the main difference will be in consistency. A good potting soil should be sifted to be of uniform texture, and will most likely be what's described as a dark black clay loam.

This will give it a high mineral content that will provide many of the essential inorganic nutrients to a planting mix. The clay loam will make it quite dense and heavy, but there's nothing wrong with this as the ultimate structure of your planting mixture can be modified by you to make one of your own choosing.

I would avoid buying a mix that is "pre-fertilized", because that takes away your own control over what type or blend of fertilizer is used in the container. And they are often more expensive than non-fertilized soils.

Soiless mixes are another possibility for using in containers. They are blends of non-soil ingredients like perlite, vermiculite and peat, the individual details of which are found later in the section called "Conditioners". They were designed initially to be used as soiless seeding mixtures.

Soiless mixes have the benefit of being very lightweight, but they can dry out quite quickly and are difficult to keep at a consistent level of moistness. For this reason I don't recommend that you use them **alone** in a container as the planting mixture. They can be added along with other ingredients as part of a planting mixture.

Composts can be from your own home compost pile, or they can be bought commercially packaged. Homemade compost is preferable, as it will likely have a much broader selection of ingredients in it, and is far less expensive. Composts are usually described as a heavy clay loam, with high humus and water content.

Good compost will contain a decomposed mixture of animal matter (from manures), vegetable matter (from kitchen and garden wastes) along with minerals such as phosphor (from rock phosphate), potassium (from wood ash) and calcium (from horticultural lime) that you've added.

Composts provide two important attributes to any planting mixture. A mix containing the ingredients mentioned above will ensure that your compost has a wide range of organic and inorganic sources of nutrients. It will also be a great source of "humus", the gummy soup that is an essential part of the soil solution mentioned before.

Conditioners are various products that will affect how your planting mixture performs, based upon the effect their structure has on the mixture. Here are the most common:

Perlite is a man-made product, made from volcanic rock that's been heat-treated to create rough lightweight white granules about the size of lentils. Because of its rough texture it holds some moisture on its surface while absorbing very little. It is relatively inert and provides no nutrients.

Its benefit in a planting mixture is that it encourages good drainage, but its lighter weight often makes it more advantageous than sand.

Sand for horticultural purposes should always be the large-grained variety from the building industry, never from a beach.

It encourages good drainage, but a sufficient amount to be of use increases the weight of any planting mix considerably.

Vermiculite is a man-made product, made from mica that's been heated until it puffs up to form lightweight granules. In the horticultural trade the granules are usually about the size of a puffed-wheat cereal or smaller. Because of its sponge-like construction, it holds several times its weight in water, as well as some air. It is quite inert and provides no nutrient value.

In a planting mix it provides pockets of air, as well as many small reservoirs of moisture that is slowly given back to the mix. It quickly reabsorbs moisture when more is provided.

Coir is a natural product, made from the fibres of the outer husk of a coconut, which is a waste product. For horticultural purposes the fibres are chopped into short lengths. The fibres absorb several times their weight in water, take a long time to break down and contain no nutrients.

In a planting mixture, coir provides lightweight water-retaining fibres that help to break up heavy soils. Since it is made from a waste product, it should be used to replace peat fibres.

Peat is a natural product, made from roots and sphagnum moss fibres that are in various stages of decomposition. It is dug up from water-filled bogs. For horticultural purposes the material is processed into short fibres. These fibres take a long time to break down, and contain very few nutrients.

Using it in a planting mix provides lightweight fibres to break up heavy soils, but it must always be kept moist because once it dries out it is difficult to re-wet.

Since peat is a resource that takes a long time to renew itself, and is used by industry in large quantities, gardeners would be environmentally wise to replace peat with coir.

Gravel

For some reason, people have the idea of using small stones or gravel as an ingredient in a container's planting mixture. They usually put a thin layer of gravel at the bottom of the container, with the idea that it somehow improves the drainage of the planting mixture.

I'd like to debunk this idea right now.

Never use a layer of gravel or small stones in the bottom of a container.

What it does is quite the opposite of improving the drainage. It actually slows the natural drainage of the planting mixture.

In a column of soil or any planting medium, whenever there's a change in the texture or structure of the material, between one type of material and another, it causes the natural downward flow of water to slow.

For example, let's look at the structure of a typical garden soil. Starting at the top there's a layer of fairly loose organic topsoil, which gets amended and planted in quite frequently. Then comes a layer of more mineral subsoil, which is not often disturbed and which is fairly compact. Below this you get to a very dense hardpan or rocks that never get disturbed at all. [Fig 12]

As water drains downwards through these various layers, whenever it comes to a transition between one layer and another it slows down and almost stops. The water starts to back up until it has built a layer that's heavy enough to burst through to the next layer, and then it continues draining.

But the funny thing about this reaction is that even if the

water is flowing downwards from a more dense to a less dense layer, it *still* slows down and builds up.

So in a container for instance, if you have a layer of gravel underneath a layer of very well drained planting mixture, the water will slow down and build up when it hits the gravel. This interferes with the good drainage that you want in the container, and you end up with a soggy wet layer just above the gravel, right where the roots are growing. This provides terrible conditions for the roots, resulting in poor growth at best and perhaps encouraging root rot in the worst-case scenario. [Fig 13] So *never, never* put a layer of gravel in the bottom of a container. If you want to make the whole container heavier to stop it from being blown over, you could mix some gravel or small stones into the planting mixture. But you've got to make sure that they're evenly distributed throughout the mixture, and NOT in a layer.

Fertilizers

Normally in a garden bed if you've used plenty of compost and organic matter, you probably don't have to feed your plants anything extra in the form of a fertilizer. There will be sufficient nutrients in the soil and sub-soil for the roots to grow around looking and finding what they need.

But in a container the situation is very different. As will be mentioned continually in this book, a container only holds a fixed amount of planting mixture. There's no big bed or sub-soil for roots to explore for more nutrients. Once the available nutrients are running low, there are *no more* available.

So if you've got a lot of plants crammed into a container, at some point they will need more nutrients than the planting mixture can naturally provide. This is where fertilizers come in handy.

You have a couple of options for adding fertilizers to a planting mixture. You can put some in right at the beginning when you make up the mixture, and you can add more later as the season progresses.

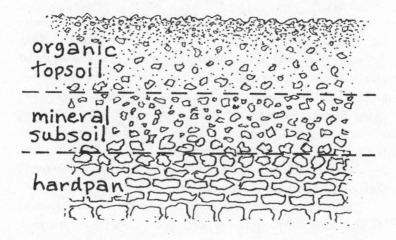

organic
topsoil

mineral
subsoil

hardpan

[FIG. 12] SOIL STRUCTURE

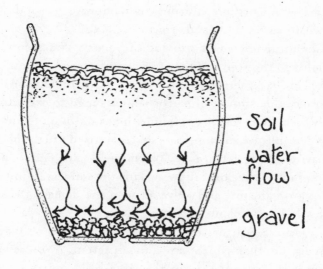

soil

water
flow

gravel

[FIG. 13] GRAVEL SLOWING WATER

For adding to the planting mixture you should use a granular slow-release type of fertilizer, so that as it gradually breaks down it can provide extra nutrients for the first few weeks of growing. For later in the season you can use a water-soluble type of fertilizer, which makes its nutrients available right away to the roots and provides an immediate boost to growth.

In both cases I would strongly recommend that you use fertilizers made from *organic* sources. I will give you the same argument in their favour as I did in my book *Stuart Robertson's Tips on Organic Gardening*.

Chemical fertilizers work, and they do make plants grow. We've known for years that a plant doesn't really care whether the molecule of nitrogen that it consumes comes from ammonium nitrate, or from horse manure.

However, the soil cares. Over the long term, the mineral salts which chemical fertilizers are made from take a toll on the life in the soil. The plants are alive, but the soil isn't, and the idea behind organic husbandry is to improve the conditions that will encourage life and growth in the soil.

Chemical fertilizers provide the macro and secondary nutrients to the soil, but they use manufactured minerals to do it. This has a serious impact on the environment, mainly because of the amount of petrochemicals used to extract and purify them. The fertilizer granules break down quite quickly in the soil and give an immediate shot of nutrients to the plants, but have less long-term value. The mineral salts tend to make the soil more saline over time, making the soil less hospitable to living organisms, and we've all seen the damage that too much salt does to plants.

Organic fertilizers definitely do require some manufacturing, but their sources are quite different. If you refer to the chart below, you can see the large-scale sources of the common elements used in organic fertilizer manufacturing. These sources are often the wastes or by-products of some other processing which would otherwise become garbage. Once processed and granulated into a fertilizer, these products break down gradually in the soil and add measured amounts of nutrients over a good part of the growing season.

So the biggest argument against chemical fertilizers and in favour of using organic source fertilizers is in the long-term impact they have on the organisms in the soil. By encouraging soil life, organic techniques build a healthy soil that in turn produces healthy plants.

~

SOME ORGANIC SOURCES
OF NUTRIENTS

~

Alfalfa meal (nitrogen)
Blood meal (nitrogen)
Bone meal (phosphor)
Cottonseed meal (nitrogen)
Crab meal (nitrogen)
Egg shells (calcium)
Feather meal (nitrogen)
Fish meal (nitrogen)
Fish bone meal (phosphor)
Granite dust (potassium)
Gypsum (calcium, sulphur)
Hoof meal (nitrogen)
Kelp (potassium)
Limestone (calcium, magnesium)
Manures (nitrogen, phosphor)
Rock phosphate (phosphor)
Shrimp meal (nitrogen)
Soybean meal (nitrogen)
Wood ash (potassium)

The granular slow-release type of organic fertilizer has yet another advantage over the same style of chemical ones. You can actually blend it into the planting mixture of a container as you put it together, **before** you put in any plants.

You cannot do this with the chemical ones. If you read the instructions on the packages of chemical fertilizers, they say to spread lightly on the **surface** of the soil so that water can gradually dissolve the chemical ingredients into the soil and slowly pass them to the roots below. This is because the chemical granules are too strong to be mixed into the soil, where the roots might contact them directly and get burned.

Fertilizers from organic sources do not have this problem. Their ingredients are much less toxic in concentrated amounts, and they break down more slowly in the planting mix. So the granules can be added to the planting mixture as you put it into the container, and end up being blended in and around the plant roots without any risk.

For more details on which fertilizers to use in your containers, see the section in Chapter Three, "Fertilizers for containers".

Mixtures for all purposes

Now that we've looked at the various ingredients that can be used in planting mixtures for containers, it's time to consider how to put them together for various purposes.

For a start, different plants can benefit from different types of planting mixtures. Some prefer heavier mineral-rich soils, and others like looser organic soils.

Then there are the situations where the weight of the planting mixture can be a factor, and the mix can be tailored to suit these purposes.

Here are recipes for a few very basic planting mixtures that I have found useful. You can alter and adjust them based upon your own experiences.

Depending on the total quantity of mixture that you're making, you can measure the "parts" with cups, scoops or shovels.

I have measured the fertilizer quantities "by the handful", because that's the way most of us tend to do it anyway, but keep the handful small.

SMALL CONTAINER MIX (e.g. 20 cm/8inch pot)
3 parts Potting soil
1 part Compost
1 part Coir/peat
1 part Perlite
1 part Vermiculite
Fertilizer (one handful)

LARGE CONTAINER MIX (e.g. window box)
4 parts Potting soil
2 parts Compost
1 part Coir/peat
2 parts Perlite
2 parts Vermiculite
Fertilizer (one handful per plant)

LIGHTWEIGHT HANGING CONTAINER MIX
1 part Potting soil
1 part Compost
2 parts Coir/peat
2 parts Perlite
2 parts Vermiculite
Fertilizer (one handful per plant)

VEGETABLE MIX
3 parts Potting soil
3 parts Compost
1 part Perlite
1 part Vermiculite
Fertilizer (one handful per plant)

PERENNIAL AND SHRUB MIX
2 parts Potting soil
2 parts Compost
2 parts Coir/peat
1 part Perlite
Fertilizer (one handful per plant/per foot of height)

SPRING BULB & HERB MIX
1 part Potting soil
1 part Compost
1 part Coir/peat
2 parts Perlite
Fertilizer (one handful per 5 large bulbs, or one handful
    per three herb plants)

If you're making up a mixture to be used in several smaller containers, I've found it best to use a separate larger container (such as a wheelbarrow or tub) in which to add the ingredients and blend them all together. Then you can fill each smaller container with the correct amount of a properly pre-blended mixture as you need it.

If you're making up a mixture for a large container, from a window box to a large planter, you can add the ingredients directly into the container itself and then stir them all together afterwards. However, I would recommend first of all adding enough ingredients to only fill half of the container, mixing them thoroughly, then adding the rest and mixing again.

CHAPTER THREE

Watering and Feeding the Container

How much water does a container need?

The amount of moisture that a container can hold will depend first of all on its size, and secondly on what type of planting mixture you're using.

When you consider that a litre of dry potting soil can absorb a half a litre of water before it gets saturated, you'll begin to realize that a container can hold quite a lot of water. All of the planting mixtures mentioned here contain other very porous ingredients as well as soil, so you can see that a container has the potential to absorb its weight in water. Fig 14]

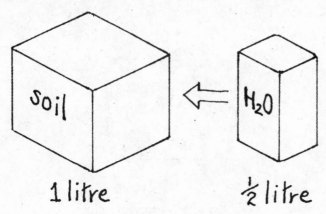

[FIG. 14] SOIL ABSORBING WATER

And as we've mentioned before, the objective of a good container and a good planting mixture is to absorb and retain as much moisture as possible for as long as possible. Our job is to make sure that containers have a consistent supply of moisture that gives them a water content between 30 and 80 percent all the time.

When you water a container, particularly a small one, you must make sure that you're soaking the whole depth of the container, otherwise you'll do more harm than good. If you add just a small amount of water, so that only the top portion of the planting mixture gets dampened, there won't be enough weight of water to soak any deeper. As a result, the smallest and most vulnerable feeder roots will head upwards towards the moist soil. This leaves them vulnerable when the surface of the planting mixture dries out, and the roots dry out too.

The object whenever you water a container is to make sure that the water soaks downwards through the column of planting mixture from the top to the bottom. Only when the whole depth of the mixture is uniformly wet will some water start running out of the holes in the bottom of the container. Then you know you've really soaked the planting mixture, and as the water drains downwards it will drag the all-essential air in behind it around the roots. [Fig 15])

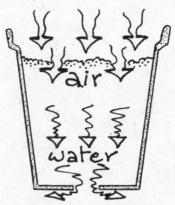

[FIG. 15] WATER/AIR FLOW

44

If you're trying to judge how much water a container needs when it's dry, pretend you're half-filling it with water. That may sound like a lot, but as mentioned before the object is to really soak the planting mixture from top to bottom. If the planting mixture is already slightly damp, it won't need quite as much water, but as long as the drain holes are clear, it never hurts to add water until it starts running out of the bottom.

The better you do this job each time, the less often you'll have to do it and the more effective it will be for the roots of the plants in the container. This applies as much to a huge planter as it does to small flowerpots.

When does a container need to be watered?

How often a container needs watering will depend on its size, how many plants there are in it and of course upon the weather.

Size The only way you'll ever know how much water a particular container needs is to experiment with it and become familiar with its look and feel.

A container that you can lift, such as a small pot or window box, should feel quite *heavy* when it's really wet. If you get to know the feel of this condition, you'll always be able to judge how damp it is and when it needs more water.

For larger containers that can't be easily lifted, you'll have to judge the soil moistness in other ways. One method is to push a thin stick or metal rod into the planting mixture so that the tip of it gets down near the bottom. As you push it in you should be able to judge the dampness of the planting mixture from the resistance, and when you pull it out you should be able to tell from its condition how damp the mixture is.

The size of a container will also influence the number and density of roots that grow in the planting mixture, and therefore how quickly the available moisture gets used up. A deep container will retain moisture longer, since not all the plants will send roots down to the bottom.

Number of plants A container that only has one shrub growing in it will obviously need less frequent watering than one with a large number of thirsty plants crammed into it. There will be considerable root competition in a densely planted container, and by the end of a growing season you can expect the planting medium to be quite choked with roots.

As the season progresses, the increasing age and size of the individual plants will also have an impact. Plants suck water up from their roots and eventually give it off from tiny holes in their leaves, in a process called "transpiration". As your plants grow and add leaves, they will transpire more water from this larger leaf area, and will suck up more water from their root system to compensate. Their roots will also grow as they get older, making it easier for them to absorb the needed water and therefore using it up faster. As the season progresses, and the plants continue to grow, they will be using up more and more water.

Weather Obviously the weather plays a critical part in how often a container needs watering. Damp rainy weather can be your friend, and hot windy conditions your enemy.

The more movement of air there is, and the higher the temperature is, the more quickly the moisture will be lifted from the leaves as they transpire. So during periods of hot weather, or even warm temperatures with windy conditions, your plants will use up a lot of the moisture available in the planting mixture. These are the times when your containers will need more frequent attention to see if they need watering.

The greater the number of leaves on your plants, the more they will be affected by the wind and the temperature. It's just a matter of mathematics; the more foliage there is, the larger the amount of leaf area that's exposed for transpiration. If the weather conditions are encouraging a high rate of transpiration, containers with large amounts of foliage will require more frequent checking to see if they need watering.

The material your container is made out of will also influence how well it holds its moisture under certain weather conditions. Terra cotta containers will dry out very quickly when exposed to the wind or sun, since they're so porous. Metal containers can heat up if exposed to the sun, particularly if they are a dark colour that absorbs the heat, drying the planting mixture more quickly inside. Solutions for both of these situations are addressed in Chapter One.

Hanging baskets full of plants are particularly exposed to the drying effects of the weather, so they can dry out quite quickly. Make sure you pay careful and frequent attention to them at all times to see if they need an extra watering. Hanging baskets can also suffer from another problem. Quite often they are set up so they're hard to reach, which makes them a nuisance

[FIG. 16] FLOODED CACHE-POT

to look after and so they get neglected. If you miss a necessary watering, even by a few hours, it can spell the end of a whole container full of plants.

The only serious problem to watch out for in times of very rainy weather is having your containers overflowing with water. If drain holes have become blocked with roots and the water is backing up, use a sharp implement to unblock the holes as soon as possible, otherwise the planting mixture will stay too wet for the health of the plants. Also, if decorative pots with no drain holes have filled up and are flooding the cache-pots hidden inside, don't let the situation stay that way. Empty the decorative containers right away so the water doesn't affect the plants. [Fig 16])

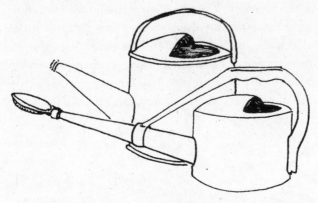

[FIG. 17] WATERING CANS

What's the best way to water a container?

There are several ways of getting the water your plants need into the containers in which they are planted. Which way you use will depend somewhat on the type of containers you have and also the number you have to look after.

Let's start with the simplest method, suitable for a moderate number of smaller containers, and that's the watering can. These should be a minimum of 4.5 litres (1 gallon) up to a maximum of about 9 litres (2 gallons). Anything smaller is not much use because it will empty too fast, and anything bigger will be too heavy to carry around. [Fig 17]

A watering can comes in useful when you want to feed your plants, because you can mix measured amounts of the water soluble fertilizer into the can very easily. But watering cans can be a problem if you have a lot of containers that are mounted or hanging above your shoulder level, as this involves a lot of heavy lifting.

For this situation, a hose with a "wand" on the end is much more practical. It's also useful if you have a lot of larger containers that would involve filling and refilling a watering can to supply them.

The "wand" is just a pipe that extends the reach of the hose. It should have an on/off tap where it connects to the hose, and on the other end there should be a "rose" or spray head that breaks up the water flow into a lot of tiny and more gentle trickles. [Fig 18]

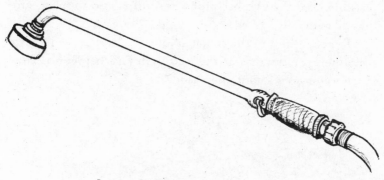

[FIG. 18] WATERING WAND AND ROSE

An even better way of watering your containers is by using a pre-installed irrigation system. This is described in more detail later in this chapter.

While on the topic of how to water a container, some consideration should be given to the actual "technique" of watering. By this I mean the actual way in which you apply water to a container. Believe it or not, there are ways to mess up watering a container, and there are ways to make it more effective.

One of the most common mistakes is to give too much water, too fast. Usually there's an inch or two of clear space between the surface of the planting mixture and the rim of the container. This area is not always sufficient to hold the correct amount of water needed by the container, so if you just slop

49

water in until it's up to the rim and then stop, you may be giving them too little.

The best way to apply water is **slowly**. If you can pour it in at about the rate at which the planting mixture can absorb it, that's perfect. I know it takes more time that way, but by doing it properly each time you can save the time of having to come back and do it more often.

If you have a lot of containers to water, one way to keep things moving is to water each of them in turn as slowly as possible, and then go back for a second round to make sure they all get really soaked.

To get an idea of the actual amounts of water needed by a container, you can refer to the section in this chapter on "How much water does a container need?"

[FIG. 19] MULCHING CONTAINERS

Mulching containers

In the same way that mulching any exposed soil surfaces saves a lot of work in the garden, mulch can be put to good use with containers also.

When you first plant up a container at the beginning of the season, there's often quite a bit of bare planting mixture exposed to the drying action of the wind and the sun. This can be fixed by simply covering the surface with a one-inch layer

50

of loose organic mulch. A couple of the best for this purpose are shredded cedar bark and cocoa bean hulls. For large planters with small shrubs or trees in them, you can also use a cover of landscape cloth spread with large bark chips.

Once you've planted up your container, and watered it really well, place the mulch all over the surface of the planting mixture. Make sure to tuck it carefully under all the foliage of the plants, so that it covers any exposed surface. [Fig 18]

The mulch will stay in place for the whole season, keeping the moisture trapped in the planting mixture much more effectively than if you allow it to be exposed to the evaporative effects of the weather. It won't interfere with watering the container, and it will actually stop a lot of dirt being splashed up onto the foliage during rainstorms.

Watering problems

When you're watering a lot of different containers, they can present certain problems that you don't run into in the garden. Here are a few things that you should watch out for as you go around with your watering can or hose.

When you water a container, it seems to take forever for the water to drain into the planting mixture. If you've used a good planting mixture that *should* drain well, then it sounds as if you've got a problem with the drain holes at the bottom of the container. If you can lift the container, poke the holes with something to clear away the roots or whatever is obstructing them. If the container is too large to lift, you'll have to work down from the surface to find the drain holes and unblock them.

As soon as you start watering a container, the water immediately starts running out of the holes at the bottom. This is usually due to the planting mixture being *too dry*. If the mixture dries out, it shrinks. This leaves a small gap between the planting mixture and the pot, all around the edge. When you pour water on the surface, it runs to the edges and drips down the sides and out of the drain holes in the bottom. Very little if any of the water gets absorbed by the planting mixture, and you're fooled into thinking that the container has been soaked because water is running out of the bottom. If you see that your planting mixture surface is dry, and there's a gap around the edges, just push your finger all around the edge to lightly fill the gap. That way, the water will be held long enough to soak into the planting mixture rather that running away. If you've covered the surface of your containers with mulch, you'll never have this problem. [Fig 19]

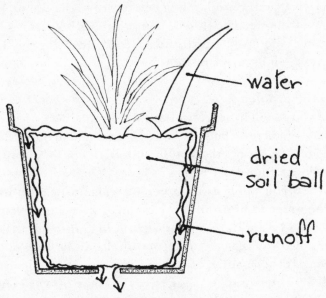

[FIG. 20] SIDE DRIP

When it rains, water fills up inside the decorative containers that don't have drain holes. This is a problem for any outdoor container that doesn't have drain holes. One answer is to hide a cache-pot **with** drain holes inside the decorative container, so that the planting mixture can always drain its excess water. But the outer un-drained decorative container can still collect rainwater, and if it fills above the base of the cache-pot you've still got a problem. The only way to solve this is to check your un-drained containers after every heavy rainfall, and empty them if necessary.

Irrigation systems for containers

As mentioned before, one of the best ways to ensure that your containers get the right amount of water all the time is to install an irrigation system designed specifically for them.

If you have a number of containers in one location, on a porch or patio for example, this is an ideal situation for an irrigation system. They are close enough together to be fed from the same supply of water, and the cost of installing the system can be minimized.

To set up an irrigation system you'll need a water tap, a solid feeder hose to get the water to the area with the containers, some thin "spaghetti" hoses to supply each container from the feeder hose, and an adjustable drip head on the end of each spaghetti hose to control the flow of water into the container. [Fig 21]

There are several models of this type of irrigation system available off-the-shelf that you can install yourself with very little skill needed. The feeder hose can usually be concealed or disguised with paint, and the spaghetti hoses are quite thin, so the whole system can be quite unobtrusive.

The secret to the system is the type of drip head on the end of the spaghetti hose that actually determines how much water flows to the container. The best types are controllable, usually by twisting them to make the opening larger or smaller. This sets the flow rate out of the drip head (often called "dribblers" or "bubblers") so that a precisely measured amount of water can be delivered in a set period of time. If the main feeder hose is connected to the tap via a water timer, you can very accurately determine just how much water is delivered, and when.

The drip head rests on the surface of the planting mixture

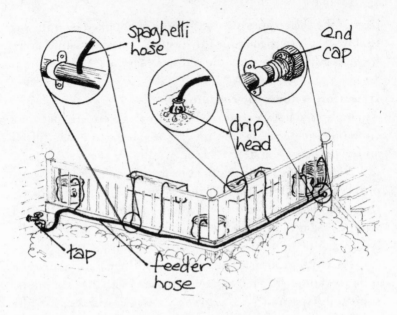

[FIG. 21] IRRIGATION SYSTEM

(just under the mulch) and feeds the root area of the plants. Each one can feed an area of about one square foot, so several can be installed in larger containers.

Containers fed with irrigation systems will seldom, if ever, need to be watered manually, and you can have the comfort of being away from your plants and knowing that they are being looked after in your absence.

Containers with reservoirs

Another watering system that is gaining in popularity involves containers with built-in water reservoirs. There are more companies making containers with this feature, and several sizes are now available.

A self-watering system is composed of a planting container filled with a regular planting mixture, and a separate base that is the water reservoir. Usually there is also an indicator of some sort to show the water level. The system allows for an upward transfer of water from the reservoir into the planting mixture above, either through direct contact via holes, or using some form of wick system. (Fig 22]

One nice feature about this method is that it gets the most moisture to the bottom of the container, encouraging the roots to penetrate deeply. Over time, some roots may even find their way into the reservoir, and adapt themselves to living in the water all the time.

Fertilizer can be added periodically to the reservoir water, but a more exact way to feed the plants in this sort of container would involve mixing the fertilizer in a watering can and applying it from the top down.

Depending on the size of the reservoir, this sort of system can save you a great deal of effort and time. As long as the reservoir never gets empty, you can be assured that the plants are getting a steady supply of water all the time. The only requirement is to regularly check the water level indicator, and refill the reservoir when needed.

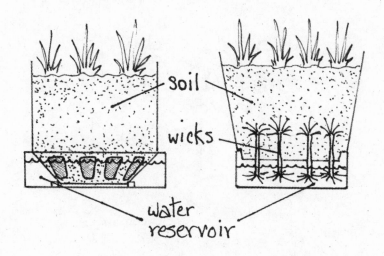

[FIG. 22] BUILT-IN RESERVOIRS

Hydroponic containers

There are some self-watering container systems that go a step further than just providing a consistent supply of water. They are classified as "hydroponic" containers, and the main difference is that they carefully supply measured amounts of water **and** nutrients to the plants. The nutrients are necessary because the plants are planted in a "soilless" growing medium.

The medium is usually completely inert, lacking any nutrients, and useful only in its ability to hold water and keep the plants upright. Hydroponic systems use media such as peat, vermiculite, rockwool cubes and porous clay pellets. These materials readily absorb moisture, and roots can easily grow through them.

Some hydroponic containers are "passive" in that they use wicks or the plant's own roots to suck up moisture. Others are "active" with pumping systems that circulate the moisture around the root area. [Fig 23, 24]

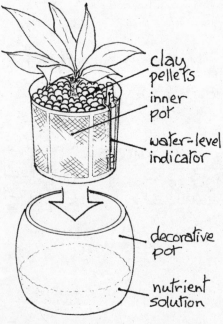

clay pellets
inner pot
water-level indicator
decorative pot
nutrient solution

[FIG. 23] PASSIVE HYDROPONIC POT

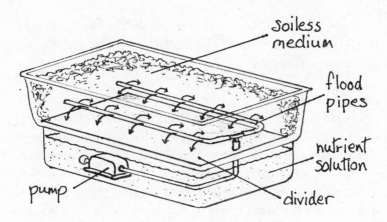

Labels: soiless medium, flood pipes, nutrient solution, divider, pump

[FIG. 24] ACTIVE HYDROPONIC CONTAINER

The critical factor in any hydroponic system is that the moisture provided to the plants is always a special "nutrient solution" of specific plant nutrients dissolved in water. This solution, rather than the planting mixture, is what provides all of the fertilizer for the plants.

Just as containers with reservoirs save time and effort, hydroponic containers reduce the maintenance workload considerably. They also provide plants with a very precise flow of nutrients and water at all times, and as a result you can achieve quite remarkable growth.

Consider vegetables such as tomatoes that respond very badly to an inconsistent water supply by splitting and developing poorly. Give them a totally consist water and nutrient flow, and they will respond by growing a more uniform harvest of fruit, as well as more of them.

The same applies to any flowering or foliage plants. A steady and consistent supply of water will allow them to grow at their best, and a regular flow of the proper nutrients will let them show their maximum potential.

While setting up hydroponic containers may have an initially higher cost, you may find the results and the reduced workload are worth it. I would suggest your first foray into hydroponics should focus on such edible plants as tomatoes, peppers and salad greens. The rewards will be quite obvious and quite tasty too!

Water crystals

There is a relatively new product on the market that is being a very big help to container gardeners. It's a polacrylamide or crystal polymer that is able to absorb large amounts of water.

What it looks like in its dry state are granules resembling large grains of sugar. But each of these tiny grains is able to absorb more that **400 times** its weight in water! And it's able to hold this volume of water, and secrete it back again later, and keep doing this over and over. So you can see its value as an additive to a planting mixture.

The crystals can last up to seven years before they break down, and they are 100% non-toxic and are completely biodegradable. They eventually break down into CO_2, water and nitrogen. Unfortunately, they are not able to tolerate freezing conditions without breaking down, so for the purposes of container gardeners in northern regions, they are only useful during one growing season.

These polymers were developed for the agricultural industry to be added to sandy soils to help plants grow in very arid climates. Their use spread to the landscaping industry to overcome similar dry conditions. More recently, the "water crystals" are being sold under various brand names to the horticultural trade, for use in gardens and containers as a way of reducing the frequency of watering needs and conserving water.

Since they can absorb so much water, they have to be used with some caution. In a test I did, I put one-half a teaspoon of dry crystals into a small 180 ml yogurt container. I added about 20 ml of water, and once the crystals had finished absorbing the water and swelling, they **filled** the container! Once they were fully swollen, they looked like perfectly clear jelly.

To take advantage of these water crystals in container gardening, the best way to use them is when you're first preparing your container. Into your empty container, add about half the planting mixture. Then sprinkle in the water crystals, stir them up a bit into the mixture, and then continue filling and planting. That way, the crystals are in the lower half of the planting mixture where the roots will be going, and where they will do the most good.

As for how much to add, this is where the caution comes in. You must NOT add too many, because they will swell up and expand the planting mixture and create a real mess, as their expansion rate in soils is around 30%. I've worked out some rules of thumb for how much to add to containers of different sizes.

CONTAINER DIAMETER	AMOUNT OF CRYSTALS
15-20cm (6-8inches)	1/2 teaspoon
20-40cm (8-15 inches)	1 teaspoon
Larger containers	1 teaspoon/sq.ft.

When you water the container, the crystals will absorb the water and stay that way until the planting mixture around them dries out enough to allow them to release their water. They will release up to 95% of their water this way, and then will re-absorb more the next time you add water.

The addition of these water crystals to a planting mixture makes an enormous difference to the length of time that the mixture stays moist. I have done tests with similar-sized containers planted with the same collection of plants. Not only did the containers with water crystals need less-frequent watering, those containers also produced plants with a noticeable advantage in the size and lushness of the foliage and flowers. This is most likely due to the consistency of water availability, but it may also benefit from the way the swollen crystals break up any compaction in the planting mixture to encourage root penetration.

These polymer water crystals have made a big difference to my container watering habits, and I would highly recommend that you make them a part of your regular planting techniques.

Watering gadgets

Over the years there have been a number of gadgets made to assist container gardeners in their watering chores. They are all designed to prolong the moistness of the planting mixture, and thereby reduce the frequency of watering. There have been mixed results with these gadgets, and you can try them for yourself.

Some of them are based around water holders planted upside down in the planting mixture, gradually releasing their water to the roots. The theory is good, but some of them let the water in so soon after a regular watering that they end up over-watering the container and not saving you any time later.

Others are based upon mats or wick systems that slowly move water from a reservoir to the planting mixture. Depending on the type of material used, and the size of the system, different amounts of water actually end up in the planting mixture. Evaporation can reduce the efficiency of these systems outdoors, as they were mainly designed for indoor use. If you were planning to rely on these during an absence, my advice would be to test them thoroughly beforehand to see if they work as planned.

As with all one-of-a-kind garden gadgets, try them first and *caveat emptor* ("let the buyer beware").

Fertilizers for containers

The plants in a container are going to need access to a good supply of fertilizer. As mentioned in Chapter One, because of the finite size of a container, the nutrients available in a planting mixture can get used up during the growing season, and will have to be replaced by you on a regular basis.

In the same way that plant density, plant size and weather

factors can affect the water consumption in a container, these factors can also affect the nutrient consumption too. Healthy active plants will demand a consistent supply of nutrients, so the more you're growing, the more you'll need to feed.

As mentioned in Chapter Two, I would advise using fertilizers made from organic sources at all times, even in your containers. There's only one problem I have with organic fertilizers, which showed up in our country garden. It appears that the smell of some of the organic ingredients, such as bone meal, can attract the likes of raccoons and skunks. The animals are tempted to dig into the containers looking for something to eat, doing quite a bit of damage to the plants in the process. This seems to happen more in the spring, when the animals are perhaps hungrier, and our plants are in their infancy. To avoid this problem, I have been forced to use organic fertilizers that do not use bone meal or seafood products. Instead, I rely on ones with super-phosphate and those from seaweed sources. I don't blame the animals, as they're just doing their job. But it's certainly frustrating to come down to the cottage and find everything dug up!

What kind of fertilizer to use

There are two types of fertilizers; *slow-release* granules, and *water-soluble* liquids or powders. The granular ones are best when added into the planting mixture at the beginning of the season when you prepare your containers. The water-soluble ones are most useful later on during the season when you need to bolster the nutrients in the planting mixture, as they can be added just by mixing them in your watering can.

Slow release granular fertilizer comes in many formulations, but the manufacturers want you to be successful with their product so they clearly mark for which type of plants they are most suitable. Whether they are organic or chemical in their sources, the formulations are very similar.

Here are a few basic fertilizer formulae. These numbers are just ratios, so the actual packages may have higher or lower numbers.

> Flowering perennials, annuals & shrubs......5-7-3
> Flowering vegetables (tomatoes, etc)..........4-7-7
> Green vegetables.................................. 7-2-2

Water-soluble liquid or powdered fertilizers are available in a couple of basic formulations, for flowering plants or predominantly green plants. They will have nutrient formulae based upon similar ratios as mentioned before for the granular ones.

When you're using these water-soluble types during the latter part of the growing season as a booster for your plants, the actual formula is not as important to your plants as the fact that you're actually adding them!

How much fertilizer to use at planting time

When you've prepared the planting mixture in your container, and before you put in the plants, you should add some slow-release fertilizer granules to provide plenty of nutrients to the plants for the first few weeks of the season.

If you're using organic fertilizer, the granules can be mixed directly into the planting mixture, as they won't burn the plant roots. If you're still using chemical fertilizer, just spread the granules on the surface after you've planted everything.

I would suggest using the following rules of thumb for adding fertilizer granules to containers:

> For **annuals**, add a small handful for each plant you're putting into the container.
> For **perennials** in a larger container, add two handfuls per plant.

*For **shrubs** in a large container, add two handfuls per square foot of planting area.*

Never put more than these amounts of fertilizer into containers. Using too much fertilizer can be toxic for your plants, and is worse than using too little. More is **not** better with fertilizers.

How to feed containers during the season

During the season, starting around the second month after the plants have been planted in their containers, I would recommend that you start feeding them **every two weeks** with a water-soluble fertilizer.

This applies to containers that are full of flowering plants, which by this time are doing very nicely and should be encouraged to keep up the good work, and to houseplants that are spending the summer outdoors.

If you're growing intensive crops of large vegetables or fast-growing vines, I'd recommend that you see the section in Chapter Five that deals with tomatoes and other big plants for special tips on feeding these crops.

If you're got planters with slower-growing shrubs in them, these probably aren't in such a drastic need of fertilizing. They can manage with the fertilizer that you mixed into their planting mixture at the start of the season. However, if these are shrubs that you've kept over the winter, and their planting mixture is more than a season old, you should definitely feed them in the spring and again in the middle of the summer with a water-soluble fertilizer.

As mentioned before, mix your water-soluble fertilizers in a watering can, carefully following the manufacturer's directions. Give a good application to each plant that you're feeding, because it's important that the fertilized water soaks right down through the planting mixture in the container, so that all of the roots have access to it.

CHAPTER FOUR

How to Select Decorative
Plants and Containers

Location, location, location

As it is with real estate, the answer to what plants to select for what situation depends entirely upon the location. And by that I'm referring to the way the specific location is exposed to **light**.

Light is the key factor in how well plants will perform if all other factors stay the same. Under the same weather conditions, watering regimes and feeding schedules, the same types of plants will perform quite differently under different light conditions.

So the first thing to consider when selecting plants for a location is **how much light that location gets**.

You have to become a judge of light levels and types of exposure. It's not that difficult once you understand what's needed by the typical categories of plants. Once you've decided what sort of light a location gets, you can start making plant selections based upon that decision.

When you're buying plants, you'll see that the growers have used identification labels for each variety. One of the most important bits of information on those labels will be the preferred light exposure. And usually they are one of **three** *basic levels; full sun, partial shade, full shade. These are often represented by symbols of a white sun, a half-black-half-white sun and a black sun.* [Fig 25]

full
sun

semi
shade

full
shade

[FIG. 25] SUN EXPOSURE SYMBOLS

Being able to judge the light levels around your growing area can therefore be based upon these three categories; full sun, partial sun and full shade. As I said, it's not that difficult.

Judging light exposure

Let's look at how to make these judgments.

First of all, **full sun** is fairly obvious. The location should be exposed to full sun for *at least* five hours a day. That means no interruptions from trees or buildings, but it could mean that your location gets full sun for three hours in the morning and then for another two hours again in the afternoon.

The **full shade** is also fairly obvious. It means that your location *never* gets exposed to direct sunlight. It may get sunlight filtered through heavy foliage or bounced off nearby walls, or it may be a northern exposure that gets no direct sun at all. Full shade will have difficulty casting a sharp shadow.

It's **semi-shade** that's the very flexible category. This sort of exposure can range from a location that gets a couple of hours of direct sun a day, to one that's exposed to the bright sky overhead or one that gets quite strong sunlight through a light layer of leaves. Semi-shade light should be able to cast a fairly good shadow at all times.

You're very likely to find that in your garden or on a deck or a balcony there will be several categories of light levels happening at the same time. One place, let's say on a wall, will be very well exposed to the sun. Another lower down in a corner could be heavily shaded. To get the best performance out of each of your plants, you'll have to consider these differences as you select plant varieties.

Having said that, you'll find that plants can be fairly flexible in their performance under not-perfect light conditions. For example, full-sun-loving geraniums can often give you quite a nice display in semi-shaded conditions if there's at least some direct sun during the day. They won't be as compact or as floriferous as they would be in full sun, but if that's the best you've got then who cares. The same thing applies when putting full shade plants into a slightly brighter location. They may do a bit better, or they may show their displeasure by growing slightly paler foliage.

For example, for years I've had a wall pot that we fill with one geranium and several impatiens. And even though these plants come from different ends of the sun exposure spectrum, they both do quite well together under the particular semi-shade conditions on that wall.

You can always push the limit a bit with light exposure, but you have to be prepared to face the consequences if you go too far. The best bet is to be quite careful when you make your main plant selection, basing it upon the light levels you expect (once all the nearby trees are in full leaf), and then you can play with the odds and ends to see how they react to what you do with them.

For a selection of plants for all types of light exposures, check the plant lists at the end of this chapter.

How does plant size affect container choice?
In container gardening, the mature size of the plants you're growing will have a bearing on what type of container you should use.

For example, if you plan on growing a small decorative tree

or a shrub in a container, it's quite likely to stay in that place for several years. So you should make sure that the container is deep enough and wide enough to hold all of the roots that the plant will want to make over time, as well as being large enough to hold sufficient planting mixture to feed and water that size of plant.

If you want to have tall vines growing out of a container, you have to realize that over the course of the season this plant will get much bigger and make a lot of roots and demand a lot of water. So the container you use should be able to accommodate these demands without causing you a lot of extra work.

Another typical example might be the case of a long container hung under a window or off a balcony railing. Invariably we want to fill them with lots of small and medium sized plants so that there's a nice display of flowers right away. But we also want the display to look nice for the duration of the season. So the box has to be deep enough to hold all of the plant roots without severe competition.

As has been mentioned in Chapter One when describing the essential specifications of a container, the *size* of the container will play a big role in how well the plants perform. So matching the container to the type of plants you're growing is going to affect the overall performance.

There are two ways you may have to approach the situation.

SITUATION A
You already own a bunch of containers, and you have to choose the plants to suit them.

In this case you have to look at each container and judge how many plants will fit into it.

Pot-shaped containers are usually about as deep as they are wide, so you have to estimate how many plants will fit in the width. A pot that narrows towards the base will have less room in it for roots than one that widens below the neck, so it can hold potentially fewer plants. You can take advantage of a very deep pot to hold a tall plant securely, whereas shallow pots should be limited to short-rooted plants. [Fig 26]

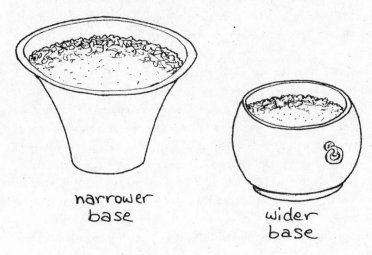

narrower base

wider base

[FIG. 26] POT SHAPES

Box-shaped containers are usually longer than they are wide, so they can end up containing a series of plants of different types and sizes. These should be grouped to make a pleasing design, with a mix of tall, short and cascading types. But you can only have this type of crowding if the box is deep enough to allow for lots of root growth over the season so that the upper growth isn't restricted. A really lush display with crowded foliage aboveground can only be achieved if the roots are not in serious competition belowground.

Other shapes and sizes of containers should be matched with plants in a way that complements the proportions of each, so they give a pleasing balance to the pairing. You also have to consider how each container and plant combination fits in with the other container and plant combinations you have, so that groupings of them have an overall cohesion to their look. [Fig 27]

[FIG. 27] GROUPING OF POTS

SITUATION B

You want to have a particular display of plants, and you have to choose a container in which to plant them.

This is really the reverse case of A) above.

If you want to have a tall elegant plant, which will be affected quite a bit by the wind, it will have to be in a deep and fairly wide container to give it stability as well as looking proportionally correct.

For a plant that's fairly short but with wide-spreading foliage, it will look good in a narrow *or* a wide pot. You can use one that's almost any shape, so your only consideration has to be that it's deep enough to hold the root ball of the plant.

When you're planning to have an arrangement of several different plants in the same container, you'll need one that has the width to give you plenty of surface area in which to plant. It can be round or rectangular and any size you like, but it must be deep enough to compensate for the crowded conditions.

In both of these situations (A and B), you'll notice that the

69

depth of the container keeps arising as an important factor. If nothing else gets through to you from this book, perhaps my repetition of this **depth** consideration will illustrate how important I think **depth** is to successful container gardening!

How to design container plantings

I don't profess to be the best teacher when it comes to laying out the design of your plants in a container. I'll never be the author of a fancy coffee-table design book on the subject. But over the years of looking at what other people have achieved, and listening to the excellent design advice of my wife, I think I can pass on some of the basic principles that seem to work.

I've split up these principles based upon the way gardeners seem to approach planning and buying the plants for their containers. If you've got other ideas, bless you! I know there are gardeners out there who have a wonderful eye for colour and texture, and who are very imaginative when it comes to mixing things together in ways that range from subtle to blatant, from studious to whimsical.

The following guides are for the people like me, who need a bit of help when it comes to actually deciding what to put in various containers, and how to have the whole collection look casually elegant, or at least suitable for the situation.

Style First of all, it seems to work well if you chose some sort of "theme" to follow with your container collection. By this I mean that if someone sees them for the first time, what sort of impression are they going to get about your style. And there are many styles or themes you could chose from, including no theme at all.

Contemporary or modern—geometric shapes and clean edges, in materials like porcelain, metal or wood, incorporating shiny or reflective surfaces, bright colours and a neat precise look.

Traditional or formal—classic sculpted shapes in terra cotta, cast iron or cement perhaps with an aged or slightly theatrical look.

70

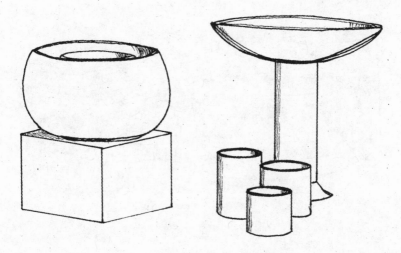

[FIG. 28] CONTEMPORARY STYLE

[FIG. 29] TRADITIONAL STYLE

[FIG. 30] RUSTIC STYLE

[FIG. 31] ORIENTAL STYLE

Mediterranean—a mix of ancient and new shapes, plenty of natural materials, and lots of strong colours.

Colonial—simple, clean and elegant lines and materials, such as painted pottery and weathered wood, with regional American touches.

Rustic or country—organic shapes made from natural materials like wood, clay and stone, with a rough and ready medieval look.

Oriental—simple lines, understated and restrained, lots of textures from natural materials, less rather than more.

Eclectic—an opportunity to mix all sorts of different looks and styles, "found" articles and recycled materials, with no apparent "theme" other than in the eye of the beholder.

These are just a few very basic styles that come to mind, and all it means is that you can keep the theme in mind when you're adding containers and plants to your collection.

For example, if your garden already has that "English country garden" feel to it, then stick with containers from the rustic or country look. If you have white stucco walls outdoors, you could use them as the basis for a Mediterranean theme. A modern condo balcony really lends itself to the contemporary or colonial look. And if all else fails, just use a bit of imagination and throw everything together and go for the eclectic look! [Fig28-31]

Colour Choosing a colour palette for your collection of flowers can be one of the most demanding of tasks. Rather like the previously mentioned "style", you should try to pick a theme for your colour scheme as well, and then stick to it and work within it.

I'm told you can make some horrible mistakes with colours, which perhaps may only be noticed by the more discerning of your visitors. But when you do get the process right, there is definitely a harmony and "pulled-together" feeling about the whole thing.

For example, colours can clash with each other, giving an

unsettled feeling. Some colours can overpower the viewer, while others can leave you feeling nothing. Colours can inspire calmness, pleasure and even passion. Colours can be used to enlarge a small space, or used to make a cozy one. Colour makes an impact, whether good or bad.

There used to be joke in our family that I was allowed to use any colour in the garden, as long as it was pink! Since then the pink phase has evolved into many other things, and with that evolution I've learned a few of the basic guidelines about planning and mixing colour.

To start with, let's understand that artists have come up with what they call a *colour wheel*. It's not quite the same as a true light spectrum, because painted (or floral) colours don't produce the same results when mixed together. It splits the colours into various names, and we'll use that convention in this book when referring to colours. The wheel also gives us a way of explaining the relationship between colours, which is important for us gardeners because it shows which ones go well together and which ones don't.

The colour wheel describes the *primary* colours (yellow, blue, red) and in between them are their mixtures called the *secondary* colours (orange, green, violet). Then in between all of those there are further mixtures called *tertiary* colours (yellow-green, blue-green, blue-violet, red-violet, red-orange, yellow-orange). [Fig 32]

Using this colour wheel to guide us, we can select colours that balance and which go well together. This is where it gets tricky, and where a bunch of "rules" come into play. The rules state that pleasing combinations can be pre-determined by using the positions of the colours on the wheel.

Complementary colours are two that are opposite each other (e.g. yellow & violet).

Adjacent colours are two that are next to each other (e.g. yellow & orange).

Analgous colours are three that are next to each other (e.g. yellow, orange, red).

74

Triad colours are three that are equidistant from each other (e.g. yellow, blue, red).

Tetrad colours are four that are equidistant from each other (e.g. yellow, blue-green, violet, red-orange).

How's that for confusing! But if you follow the colours around the wheel and look at the combinations, you'll see the logic behind it. After that, you have to try and understand (or just accept) that these combinations actually **do** work, and that others tend to bring about colour clashes. [Fig 33]

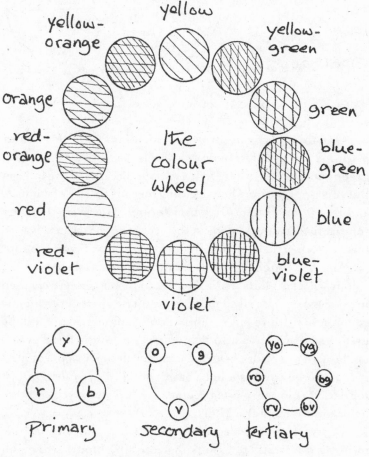

[FIG. 32] COLOUR WHEEL

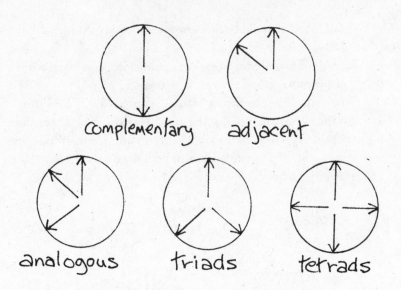

[FIG. 33] COLOUR COMBINATIONS

One thing that can throw a wrench into all of this colour planning and use of the colour wheel is the fact that the colour **green** appears everywhere in the garden, because of the foliage. But you can ignore it when deciding on your palette of colours, and treat it as a rather dark background. However, there are some foliage colours, such as the greys and variegated leaves, that you can actually bring into the colour mix if you want to.

Another "oddball" colour, one that doesn't appear in the colour wheel at all, is **white**. But it can be very effectively used in your palette. Because of its neutrality, it pairs up with any colour and fits into any combination of colours. White can be used for its brightness, to lighten areas or to catch the eye. It can be used as a bridge between areas of pale and bright colours. It can also be used as a light background to provide contrast for darker colours. White becomes the "universal" colour that helps out in many situations.

Now that we've looked at the colour wheel, we can continue to break down other reasons that certain colours work well together.

There are **hot** colours, and there are **cool** colours.

The hot ones really stand out and catch the eye. They retain their colour dominance even under the most sunny conditions that wash the strength out of weaker colours. The hot ones are the strong primary colours such as red, yellow, orange.

The cool colours are less startling to the eye, and are colours such as pink, green and blue. They can be washed out by strong sunlight, so they do best growing more in the shade.

Within any colour, there are **tints** and **shades**.

Tints are the lighter version of any colour. Think of a colour with white added. Red with white gives you pink, blue with white gives you lavender. Tints are more reflective, and give a sense of openness.

Shades are a darker version of any colour. Think of a colour with black added. Red with black gives you scarlet, blue with black gives you purple. Shades are less reflective, and give a more closed feeling.

So this means that you can mix either red and yellow or pink and yellow, because pink is a "tint" of red and is still in the same colour family.

Now that we've discussed the actual colours, their combinations and their attributes, it's time to look at some of the tricks that can be used when choosing and mixing colours.

Contrast is the balance of light and dark against each other. The eye compares the difference, and the brain can be fooled into various perceptions. For example, lighter colours appear closer, while darker ones appear further away. Light colours (of anything from blooms to a pathway) can be used to highlight an area against a darker background. A short garden can be "lengthened" by using light colours closer to the viewer and darker ones further away. Lighter foliage colours behind darker blooms can help the blooms to stand out. A dark shrub separating two bright, but not-quite-matching-colours, can help them seem more alike.

Distance affects the impact of colours. It mutes the effect of strong colours, so you can use this to either soften bright colours by planting them further away, or to keep their impact by planting them closer. On the other hand, light colours are able to draw the eye over longer distances, so they should be used to brighten distant views and to force the viewer to look further.

Low light levels in areas can be overcome up by the use of lighter colours. If you want to dispel the gloom in locations where foliage or buildings create heavy shade, use containers and plantings in light colours to brighten up the area. Don't forget that light grey or variegated foliage can just as bright as some flowers.

Surface texture plays a role in the way colours are perceived. For example, containers and plant foliage with rough textures will absorb light, making them seem darker and further away. Smooth surfaces on containers or foliage have the opposite effect, as they reflect a lot more of the light and seem brighter and closer.

Directing the viewer to look somewhere specific can be done in several ways. You can get the most impact right away by using the most vivid colours, either close-up or at a distance. As already mentioned, it can also be done using light colours at a distance or by using the contrast of a dark background to highlight a lighter colour in front. Then there's the trick of using a line of light colours, such as path or a series of bright plants in containers, to draw the eye along its length to a visual goal at the end. [Fig 34]

Creating harmony is perhaps the opposite of trying to direct the viewer. Here the objective is to provide a pleasing flow of colour that avoids any sudden impacts and eye-catching devices. The best way to achieve this is first of all to use colours that all have about the same brightness value, where no single colour stands out or dominates. And secondly, to use colours that blend together because they respect the "rules" of colour mentioned before. They combine because they are Complementary, Adjacent, Analogous, Triad or Tetrad. Sticking closely

[FIG. 34] LEADING THE EYE

to these rules and avoiding dominant colours will keep the whole package harmonious to the eye. If you want to create a restful atmosphere, use cooler pastel tints throughout. For a more vibrant feeling, while still being harmonious, use a collection of the brighter and more vivid hot shades.

And don't forget that **time** can play tricks in the garden too. As plants change during the season, they can also change their colours. Whether it's a plant that finishes blooming and then becomes a "green" plant, or foliage that suddenly turns bright red in the autumn, the colours of each individual plant at each stage of its growth must be taken into consideration in your colour scheme.

Shape Using the "shapes" of containers, plants and even particular foliage is also an important part of designing container plantings.

The shape may tie in with a particular style, such as a contemporary look with geometric shaped containers and large round foliage. Or it may help to follow a theme you're establishing, where everything is in loose flowing lines with plants that have gracefully arched foliage and containers have ornately curved embellishments. Shape may even help you overcome problems you associate with the layout of your growing area.

For instance, in a very shallow but wide growing area or one with overhead obstructions, perhaps you want to create a feeling of more height. To do this you could use containers that are tall and rather thin, along with tall plants that have long narrow foliage and accentuate their height, particularly if they are positioned in the corners of the view. This creates vertical lines that fool the eye into thinking "height".

In quite the opposite situation, if your space is rather tight and open to the sky making it feel "small and tall"; you need to use the opposite shapes. Your containers and plants should be shorter and wider, keeping the eye closer to the ground. If you also use containers and flowers that have similar colours and levels of brightness placed side by side, the eye will roam from side to side and the brain will think "width", rather than looking up. Shape can also help to create a feeling of lushness, even in a very small area that only has room for a few plants. By using plants that all have foliage in distinctly different shapes and sizes, from spiky blades and elaborate filigrees to rounded hearts and tiny sprays, the eye sees enough variety to keep it busy.

Flower heads have shapes too, which can by used to either increase the variety or harmonize with each other. There are the flat heads of daisies and cosmos, the large sprays of lobelia and bacopa and the trumpet-like shapes of petunia and lavatera.

So shape can play a part in the selection and variety of what you put into containers, as well as the containers themselves having their own distinctive shapes.

Height Using height as part of your planting design is yet another element in how things end up looking. We've mentioned using tall plants in various situations, but there are other elements to height as well.

In some planting locations, walls are a dominant feature. They can sometimes be an obstacle, but they can also be used to advantage.

Many plants can be "convinced" to climb up a wall, particularly if they are offered some support. The vines such as clematis, cardinal creeper, morning glory and jasmine will all grow several feet in a season if they have something substantial to climb around as they grow. A suitably large-sized container on the ground will provide the moisture and nutrients, and netting or a wooden trellis will guide them upwards. Even non-vines such as nasturtium will spread upwards if trained on some support.

When you don't have a lot of room to grow things, any available vertical space should not be wasted. If you don't grow things up it, you can always use wall pots to allow plants to grow downwards.

The look of plants cascading out of a container is always nice, and many plants that would normally be thought of as "upright" can be coaxed into tumbling over the edge. For instance, plants like alyssum and mimulus that cover a lot of ground in the garden can cascade with great abandon when used in a container. Even geranium, begonia and impatiens can be encouraged to cascade if the stems are gently pushed over to grow outwards rather than upwards.

Of course there are the plants that are used most often for their downward-growing habit, such as *vinca major, solanum jasminoides* (star of Jerusalem) and *petunia*. These plants have no trouble arching their stems out and down as they grow.

Using the height of plants to create an arrangement of taller and shorter flowers and foliage will be dealt with in the next section.

Arrangement

The actual arrangement of various plants in a container is another activity that demands a bit of skill. There are so many "looks" that can be created by the selection and layout of plants that I can't hope to cover them all. But I'll try and mention a few of the more obvious ones.

If a circular pot is to be seen from all sides, it should be planted so that there's really no "best" side. Usually you'll have something taller in the centre, with a collection of shorter and cascading plants arranged around the rim.

If the same pot is positioned up against something so that there's one part that will be somewhat hidden, you can arrange the same selection of plants in a different way. The taller plant can be in the centre-rear, with the other smaller plants positioned to the front and sides. [Fig 35]

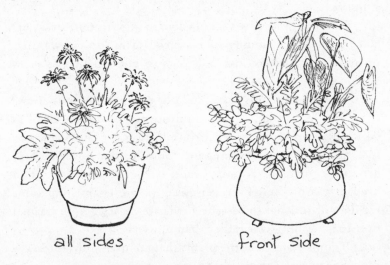

all sides   front side

[FIG. 35] FRONT AND SIDE ARRANGEMENTS

Let's say you have a very large plant, like a small shrub or a rose bush, in a large planter. Because a lot of the surface of the planting mixture below will be exposed, you should certainly cover it with mulch. But you can also allow low growing plants

to cover the surface as a much more attractive "living mulch".
You can use ground covers such as *vinca minor* or *lamium*,
and other annual low growers like *alyssum* or *mesembryanthemum*. If the shrub is staying in the pot from year to year, you
could also use creeping perennials such as *phlox subulata* or
thymus. [Fig 36]

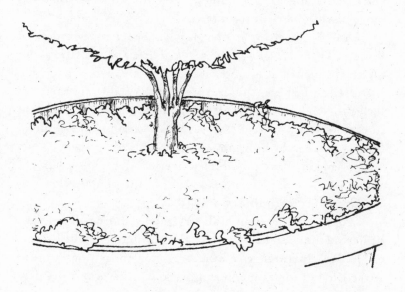

[FIG. 36] LIVING MULCH

One frequently used type of container where the arrangement of the plants is important is the window box. Since this
is usually a long rectangular shape, the individual plants need
to be planned to work well together. You can arrange the
different plant varieties so that they stay in separate clumps, or
you can make sure their foliage and flowers become intertwined
and blended together. And window boxes usually have plenty
of downward vertical room for cascading plants to be seen, so
they should be planted near the edges so they can fall over and
grow downwards. [Fig 37]

Speaking of cascading plants, hanging baskets are a type of container that really show off the effect of plants dangling over the edge. Some baskets just have plants such as *fuchsia* or *petunia* planted in the centre so they arch outwards and downwards as they grow. There are other types of baskets that have shorter plants such as *impatiens* planted in the top and also stuck in the sides through holes, so that the finished job looks more like a "globe" of flowers.

And a relatively new concept is the hanging "cylinder" of flowers. This is usually a tube made of heavy plastic film about 45 cm (18 inches) long and about 15 cm (six inches) wide that is stuffed full of planting mixture. Small plants are then inserted through slits in the plastic so their roots rest in the mixture. The result after a few weeks is a column of colourful flowers that can be hung anywhere suitable. [Fig 38]

For more ideas on which varieties of plants to use in containers, see the "Plant Lists" later in this chapter.

Grouping containers

Large containers can look very good standing alone, particularly if the container has attractive details or embellishments on it. Well-planted containers can be individually quite attractive, but sometimes having a group of several containers put together can have more of a visual impact.

Small pots in particular look a bit lost sitting on their own, whereas a group of three or four look as if they were intended to be where they are. There's also another advantage to having several small pots close together, as they tend to create a small microclimate of higher humidity around themselves, thereby reducing the need for watering quite so often. [Fig 39]

However, when putting several containers together you have to take into consideration how the members of the grouping suit each other. There has to be some "theme" to the collection, or at least they have to go well together. The same thing applies to the plants used in this grouping of different containers. There has to be some visual balance and cohesion to the choice

[FIG. 37] CASCADING WINDOW BOX

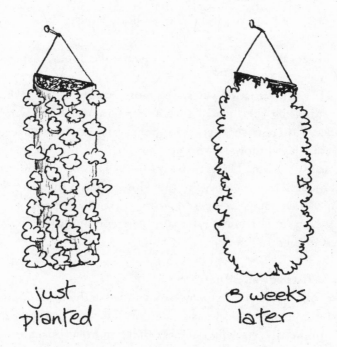

just planted

8 weeks later

[FIG. 38] COLUMN OF FLOWERS

[FIG. 39] GROUP OF SMALL POTS

of flowers and foliage, whatever the mix of colours, shapes and textures.

The one situation where the most care should be taken in coordinating the look of several containers is with window boxes. If there is a collection of them along a railing, or several gracing the windows of a home, they should either match or be of a similar style. This doesn't mean they have to be identical, although that looks nice. But they should have a theme to their shape and colour scheme, something that pulls the look of them together. And of course, the same concepts apply to the plants used in them.

Plant lists for all situations

The following lists are to give you an idea of the types of plants that can be used in various situations. They are by no means a comprehensive list of all plants or all combinations, and a lot of what you end up doing should come from your own trial and error.

Light exposure

As with all planting situations, light exposure is the first key consideration when choosing what plants to place where. For a better description of how to determine what constitutes the three basic divisions of light exposure, you can refer to the section on "location" at the beginning of this chapter.

Don't forget that you can often get quite good results from plants listed in a category when they are exposed to light conditions slightly better or worse than what is preferred.

As with all perennials and shrubs, remember to check that the plants you choose are suitable for your zone.

Flowering annuals, perennials and small trees & shrubs
FULL SUN

ANNUALS	PERENNIALS	SHRUBS
Alyssum maritimum	Artemesia (many)	Berberis thunbergii
Angelonia	Calluna	Calluna
Bidens	Cerastium	Datura
Calibrachoas	Chrysanthemum (many)	Forsythia
(Million Bells)	Geum chiloense	Genista
Canna lily	Heuchera	Juniperus dwarf
Capsicum frutescens	Lavandula spica	Picea dwarf
Celosia argentea	Ornamental grasses	Pinus dwarf
Chaenorrhinum	Salvia superba	Potentilla fruticosa
Dahlia	Saponaria	Paeonia
Dorotheanthus	Sempervivum	Ricinus
Euphorbia	Veronica spicata	Rose
Gaillardia pulchella		Ruta graveolens
Gazania		Spirea bumalda
Gypsophila elegans		Yucca
Helianthus hybrids		
Heliotrope		
Lavatera		
Linaria maroccana		
Melampodium		
Nemisia		
Osteospermum		
Papaver		
Pelargonium		
(geranium)		
Petunia hybrida		

ANNUALS	PERENNIALS	SHRUBS
Plumbago		
Portulaca		
Sanvitalia		
Scaveola		
Schizanthus		
Thymophilla		

SEMI-SHADE

ANNUALS	PERENNIALS	SHRUBS
Ageratum	Achilliea (many)	Abies dwarf
Anchusa capensis	Armeria	Abutilon
Arctotis	Aubretia	Buxus (Box)
Aster (callistephus)	Bellis perennis	Cephalanthus
Bacopa	Campanula	Chamaecyparis
Brachycome	Coreopsis grandiflora	Comptonia
Browallia	Euphorbia -	Cornus alba
Calendula	polychroma	Cotoneaster
Celosia	Hemerocallis	Euonymus alatus
Coreopsis tinctoria	Iberis sempervirens	Hydrangea
Cosmos	Lamium	Ilex (Holly)
Dianthus barbatus	Myosotis	Persicaria
Diascia	Platycodon	Rhododendron &
Dimorphotheca	Sedum spectabile	azalea hybrids
Eustoma	Viola cornuta	Sorbaria
Hibiscus		Stephanandra
Iberis umbellata		Thuja dwarf
Lobelia		Viburnum trilobum
Matricaria eximia		Weigela
Mirabilis jalapa		
Nicotiana alata		
Nierembergia		
Phlox drummondii		
Salvia splendens		
Tagetes (Marigold)		
Thunbergia		
Torenia fournieri		
Tropaeolum majus		
Verbena hybrida		
Viola hybrida		
Zinnia elegans		

ANNUALS	PERENNIALS	SHRUBS
SHADE		
Begonia (many)	Astilbe chinensis	Aruncus sylvester
Campanula isophylla	Bergenia	Cotinus coggygria
Coleus	Campanula pusilla	Leucothoe
Fuchsia	Ferns	Mahonia
Impatiens	Hosta	Microbiota
Mimulus hybrids	Lamium	Taxus (Yew)
Kochia	Vinca	

Climbing plants

Vertical spaces are valuable growing spaces, and containers can provide a "home" for all sorts of annual and perennial climbers. Nearly all of the ones mentioned will do best if given a full sun exposure, and they will all require some support system to climb up.

Check Chapter Six for more information on supporting climbing plants.

ANNUALS	PERENNIALS
Asarina	Akebia quinata
Cobea scandens	Aristolochia (Dutchman's pipe)
Dolichos lablab	Campsis radicans
Ipomea (morning glory)	Celastrus scandens
Lathyrus (sweet pea)	Clematis (hybrids)
Mandevilla	Humulus (hops)
Mina lobata	Hydrangea anomala
Passiflora	Lonicera japonica (honeysuckle)
Quamoclit (cardinal climber)	Parthenocissus (Virginia creeper)
Thunbergia alata	Polygonum aubertii
Tropaeoleum (nasturtium)	Shisandra chinensis
	Vitis (grape)
	Wisteria

Foliage plants

These are garden plants that are known mostly for their foliage rather than their flowers.

Alternanthera, brassica (kale), coleus, colocasia (elephant ears), cynara (cardoon), dichondra, dracaena, ferns, hedera (ivy), helichrysum, hyposestes, kochia, juncos, ornamental grasses, senecio cineraria (Dusty Miller), stachys lanata (lamb's ears).

Bulbs

Although most spring and summer bulbs have a fairly short blooming time, they should not be left out of container planting schemes. Many have attractive foliage which remains long after the blooms have faded, and some will stay in bloom for quite a long time under cool and shady conditions.

For the spring-blooming bulbs, you can consider dedicating containers to them specifically, and then removing the bulbs when they have finished to be replaced with other plants.

The summer-blooming bulbs should be included as part of your summertime container plant arrangements, and be planted in the spring. (See Chapter Six for planting details)

Most spring and summer bulbs prefer full sun or partial sun exposure to do their best. Don't forget that in the very early spring, when spring bulbs are in bloom, there is potentially more sun exposure because the deciduous trees have not yet grown their leaves. So a normally shady location may be sunny enough for a container of spring bulbs.

SPRING BULBS	SUMMER BULBS
Allium	Achimenes
Anemone blanda	Agapanthus
Camassia	Allium (many varieties)
Chionodoxa	Begonia (many varieties)
Crocus (many hybrids)	Caladium
Fritillaria	Canna lily
Galanthus (snowdrops)	Cyclamen
Hyacinthus	Dahlia
Iris reticulata	Gloriosa (climbing lily)
Muscari ornithogalum	Liatris
Narcissus (many incl. daffodil)	Lilium (many varieties)
Scilla	Nerine bowdenii
Tulipa (many varieties)]	Oxalis
	Ranunculus (many varieties).

Tender shrubs

There are several shrub-like plants that are not hardy enough to withstand being left outside for sub-zero winters. They grow much larger than the average houseplant, and some are valued for their blooms as well as their foliage.

If these plants are to be saved from one year to the next, they need to be brought indoors out of the cold for the duration of the winter. They can be stored in a very cool location, to be left dormant for the winter. Or they can be given a warm and sunny location to continue growing, and even blooming, throughout the winter.

Azalea, camellia, citrus, hibiscus, nerium oleander, orchid hybrids, palms.

Houseplants

All of your houseplants will benefit from spending the summer months outdoors, as long as they are kept in shady conditions and not exposed to the direct sun, to which they are not suited.

They will grow quite vigorously during their stay in the brighter light conditions experienced outside, and they will face a whole new set of weather conditions.

As a result, you should expect to be watering and feeding them on a different schedule than they were on indoors. Watering will to some degree be dictated by the weather conditions, as explained in Chapter Three, and may be more frequent than normal. And because they are growing better, they will also need to be fed once a month throughout the summer.

You may also realize that the plants could do with being re-potted at some point during the summer. Sure signs of this are if you see a lot of roots growing out of the bottom of the container, or the planting mixture seems to be drying out very quickly because the pot is full of roots. Just tip the plant out of its container, cut away about 20 percent of the root ball from around the outside and the bottom, and re-pot the plant with new planting mixture [Fig 40]

[FIG. 40] RE-POTTING HOUSEPLANT

Your houseplants can be kept in their regular containers, or given newer more decorative ones for the summer. But remember that all of these containers must drain really well, because being out in the rainy weather will expose them to much more water that they are used to indoors.

Your houseplants will probably grow a lot of new foliage while they are outside during the summer months. That's because of the higher light levels they will be exposed to. Unfortunately, this will all change when you bring the plants back indoors at the end of the summer. The light levels indoors will be much lower, so don't be surprised if they react to this change by dropping off some of their older leaves. This is quite a natural "pruning" process.

Colour schemes

As described earlier in this chapter, colour plays a very important role in selecting the plants for your containers. Not only is the balance between specific colours important, but so are things like the contrasts of light and dark, the textures of the foliage and the "feel" that these colours create.

You really have to make your colour decisions before you even decide which plants to buy. Once the colours are decided upon you can then make the next level of decisions on which varieties to use (with those colours), and how to place them. But colour comes first.

I would suggest that you keep it simple at first, and then get more complex as you gain experience and confidence in using colour. Pick two or three colours that go well together, and then see what sort of plant selection this gives you.

For example, for a window box in a semi-shaded location let's say you choose blue, pink and white as your principal colours. With those in mind you can start to list your annual plant options.

In the blue family you could use *ageratum, anchusa capensis, aster, browallia, calendula, lobelia* and *nierembergia.*

In pink you've got *aster, bacopa, brachycome, cosmos, dianthus, diascia, eustoma, iberis, mirabilis, nicotiana, phlox, salvia, verbena* and *zinnia.*

In white there are *bacopa, brachycome, browallia, calendula, dianthus, diascia, dimorphotheca, eustoma, iberis, lobelia, matricaria, mirabilis, nicotiana, phlox, torenia* and *verbena.*

Within this selection there are tall and short plants, cascading plants and spreading plants. You've got a wide range of styles that all fit into the colour choices you want for your particular light exposure. All you have to do is select which plants go in which places within the window box.

Here's an example of how you could arrange these plants in a window box. [Fig41]

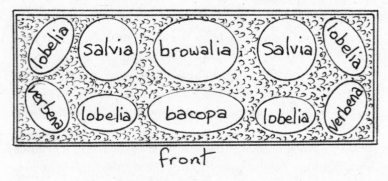

[FIG. 41] WINDOW BOX PLANTING PLAN

In another example, using a large round container located in the full sun, let's suppose we choose a pairing of hot colours such as red and yellow. Here are some of the plant options for this planting situation using annuals.

In red, you could select from *calibrachoas, celosia, papaver, pelargonium* (geranium), *petunia, portulaca, salvia* and *zinnia.*

In yellow there are *bidens, calibrachoas, dorotheanthus, gaillardia, gazania, helianthus, petunia, portulaca, rudbeckia,* and *sanvitalia.*

Again, you have a selection of different heights and spread to choose from, and here's an example of how some of these plants could be put to use. [Fig42]

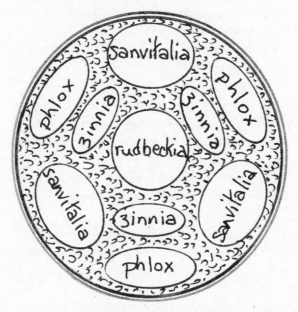

[FIG. 42] ROUND PLANTER PLANTING PLAN

You may even find that you have a situation where you've got some containers in full sun, while others in another location are getting much less sun exposure. This obviously means that you have to select different varieties of plants for each area. But that doesn't mean that you have to have a different colour scheme altogether.

You can take advantage of the shadier area to use colours that are 'tints", or slightly paler and pastel versions of your selected colours. Then in the sunnier area you can use the stronger "shades" of those same main colours to overcome the stronger light they're exposed to.

For example, using the colours pink and yellow as your overall scheme you can modify them for sun and shade. In the shade you can use a delicate pale pink *begonia* along with the lightest version of a lemon yellow *mimulus*. In the sun, try two much stronger versions of the same colours such as a shocking pink *petunia* with a golden yellow *gaillardia*. Overall you've followed the same colour-pairing rules, but you've used different versions from the same colour families to compensate for the light exposure.

When you're selecting the colour palette for your container plants, you should also take into consideration any other colours there are around. If you have in-ground flowerbeds, their colours must be part of the mix. And don't forget things like the colours of walls, fences, painted furniture or fixtures and even background tree and shrub foliage.

This sort of colour management allows you to make decisions based upon all the colours in use throughout a garden. This gives the whole area a harmonious appeal, because the eye is not forced to deal with jarring colour notes or disjointed mixes.

That doesn't mean that you can't be bold in your choice of colours and effects. But even boldness has to fit in to the scheme of things, either as a "statement" or as an overall impression.

Colour scheme ideas can come from all sorts of places. I remember one talented gardener who selected her palette by following an Impressionist master. She had always been fascinated by a springtime painting by Monet, of his Japanese bridge located in his garden at Giverny in France. She took note of all the subtle colours of the flowers, foliage and even reflections in the water, and used them as the basis for her garden flowers. Everything she planted used that particular range of colours, and since they were so pleasing in the painting, they ended up being very pleasing in the garden.

Perhaps the most difficult thing about choosing the colour palette to use in a specific planting situation is the enormous choice of colours that are available in the plant world. When you walk down the aisles of a garden centre, there are all these wonderful colours calling out to you to be used. But this is where you have to have some sort of plan up your sleeve.

If you know the sun exposure you're buying for, that eliminates a certain number of plants right away. Then you have your pre-determined selection of colours listed, and this is where you have to *stick to the plan*. Don't get sidetracked by an adorable little red flower if what you're looking for is pink. Be strong, take note of it for another year, and then move on.

Then grab some of the plants that are on your list, and after you've collected a few, lay them out and see how they fit together from a colour point of view. This is also the time to make sure you've got the right mix of tall, short and cascading style plants for your particular containers. Don't be shy to play around while you're shopping. It might be nice if you don't do your dithering at lunchtime on a busy Saturday in the spring, but most garden centres won't mind you messing around with plants in order to get things right.

Then, once you've made your colour and plant decisions, you can figure out how many you need of each one and put your selection together. It's always wise to buy a few *more* plants than you think you need, for several reasons. First of all, you may have erred in your estimates of what's needed. Secondly, you may lose a few plants to weather, carelessness or acts of God. And thirdly, if you go back to buy more for replacements, there might not be any more left of that exact plant.

Don't forget to try and follow the colour blending advice that was mentioned earlier in this chapter. It's all based on the colour wheel, and the relationships between the various strengths of colours. There are good reasons why certain colours go well together and others seem to clash, and for anyone needing advice on mixing colours, it's a good place to start.

Some colour schemes to avoid

Pairing hot and cool colours in a small area like a window box. (It makes the cool colours almost disappear as the eye is drawn to the hot colours.)

Mixing pastel and vivid colours too close together. (This also draws the eye to the vivid colours, and the pastel ones tend to be forgotten.)

Using dark-coloured flowers and foliage in dark areas. (This is a recipe for the container and its contents to never be seen, so unless you're into a camouflage look, don't pair dark with dark.)

Using pale-coloured flowers and foliage in very bright locations. (With strong sun always beating down, your pale colours will be washed out and any subtlety will be lost.)

Combinations

In this section, I've put together a few plant combinations that you might like to try if you're looking for ideas. They are far from the only mixtures that are possible, but they've all been tried and shown to work quite nicely.

The combinations have been divided up into container types, so that you can select them based on the amount of space you have. Within each container type it's again divided by sun exposure, to give you some ideas on which plants are available to be combined.

Window boxes

FULL SUN

1. *Pelargonium* down the middle, with *osteospermum* and *sanvitalia* mixed together at either end, and *scaevola* and *petunia* cascading over the front.

2. *Gaillardia* and short *helianthus* down the rear of the box, with *calibrachoas* spilling out all along the front.

SEMI-SHADE

1. *Browallia* along the back, with *matricaria* and *zinnia* in

front of it, and *verbena* and *dimorphotheca* spilling over the front with their foliage intertwined.

2. *Nicotiana* in the middle, surrounded by *brachycome* and *nierembergia*, with some *lobelia* hanging over the edges.

3. *Coreopsis* and *calendula* mixed in the rear, with *diascia* and *verbena* growing up and out along the front.

SHADE

1. *Coleus* in the centre, with *begonia* filling the rest and falling over the front.

2. *Campanula isophylla* along the rear, with *impatiens* around it and *mimulus* cascading over the sides.

Large pots

FULL SUN

1. *Canna lily* in the centre, with *lavatera* and *dahlia* planted around it, and some *schizanthus* growing over the edges.

2. *Pelargonium* rising from the middle, with *calibrachoas* all around the outside and falling over the edges.

3. *Oranmental grass* clump in the center, surrounded by *melampodium* and *osteospermum* around the edges.

SEMI-SHADE

1. *Salvia splendens* in the centre, with *thunbergia* and *brachycome* surrounding it and falling over the sides.

2. *Mirabilis jalapa* growing in the middle, with *bacopa* and *diascia* tumbling over all the edges.

3. *Buxus* shrub in a round shape, surrounded by *matricaria* and with a few *verbena* growing over the sides.

SHADE

1. *Begonia* (large variety), with *mimulus* and *impatiens* allowed to grow over the edges.

2. *Campanula isophylla* and *mimulus* mixed together and allowed to mingle their foliage.

Planters

FULL SUN

1. *Rosa rugosa* (small shrub) under-planted with a living

mulch of *alyssum maritimum*.

2.*Ricinus* (castor bean plant) surrounded by a mix of *melampodium, celosia plumosa* and *bidens*.

3.*Sprirea bumalda* in the centre, with *nemisia, scaevola* and *osteospermum* in a mix around the edges.

SEMI-SHADE

1.*Persicaria* in the centre rear, with *cosmos* and *nicotiana alata* around it in front, and *nierembergia* cascading over the front edge.

2.*Dwarf thuja* in the centre, surrounded by a mix of *coreopsis tinctoria* and *calendula,* with *thunbergia* falling from the sides.

3.*Sedum specatabile* and *salvia splendens* mixed together to fill the centre, with *verbena* and *diascia* tumbling over the edges.

SHADE

1.*Taxus* shrub, trimmed to an urn shape, surrounded by *coleus*.

2.*Cotinus coggygria* in the rear, surrounded by mixed *hosta* varieties with variegated leaves.

CHAPTER FIVE

Growing Food in Containers

Growing food in containers

Containers are not just useful for growing decorative plants. Just like your garden beds, containers can be used to grow vegetables and herbs to be used in the kitchen too.

If your only gardening space is a sunny balcony or deck, you don't have to give up hope of eating fresh homegrown tomatoes and salad greens. Any vegetables and herbs that you like can be grown in the right containers and under the right conditions. Whether it's a single basil plant in a pot or a tomato in a planter, edible plants are quite at home in containers.

And for gardeners who don't have room for full-scale vegetable production in their regular decorative garden, a few containers can help you grow a selection of tasty treats instead.

The following guidelines are divided up into *herbs, large vegetables,* and *small vegetables.* They're divided up this way to reflect the different planting mixtures that each group would prefer. These mixtures are mentioned in Chapter Two, but are reprinted here as well for your convenience.

Remember that all your of containers will hold their moisture longer if they are made of non-porous materials. Terra cotta pots should be coated with a water-sealant or lined with plastic. Your containers will also stay moister longer if you mulch the surface of the planting mixture. (See Chapter One)

Herbs

This group is one of the easiest and most satisfying to grow of all the edible plants. They take very little skill to get great results, and you can use them fresh in your cooking throughout the season. You can even prolong the pleasure of homegrown herbs by either preserving your own harvest for use during the winter months, or growing a selection of herbs indoors during the winter.

The care and maintenance requirements of the herbs mentioned in this chapter are very much the same as those for the decorative annual and perennial plants mentioned in the first few chapters. They need to be watered, fed, deadheaded and generally cared-for in much the same way as any foliage and flowing plants. All these herbs will do best of you grow them in full sun conditions, but many will still give you decent results in half-sun.

In reward for this care and attention, you'll reap a harvest of useful and flavourful material for your home.

Containers for herbs You can grow individual herbs in their own individual containers, such as small terra cotta pots, but remember that you'll run into the same problems as with any small pots of keeping them watered throughout the season. While small containers may be quite useful, for moving around and grouping for their ornamental appeal, they can be a nuisance to maintain.

Sometimes it's worth considering setting up a larger container, such as a window box, filled with a selection of your favorite culinary herbs. This makes even more sense if you locate it within easy reach of the kitchen, to avoid pre-mealtime trips far into the garden during rainstorms.

One particularly interesting container for a collection of herbs is the Mexican strawberry pot. It's tall and narrow, usually about 45cm (18inches) high, and 25cm (10inches) at its widest. It has a series of cup-like openings all around it, into which the small plants are planted. It was originally designed to allow strawberry runners to cascade down from each cup, but it makes a great herb container too. You can plant a different herb in each cup, giving you at least a dozen choices, and they'll drape themselves all over the pot. It's very handy near the kitchen. [Fig 48]

window box   strawberry pot

[FIG. 48] HERB PLANTERS

Some annual herbs that grow into quite tall plants such as basil, borage or parsley, can be grown in their own large containers. This way they'll have plenty of room to spread and reach their full potential, as well as looking attractive on their own in a container.

All the perennial herbs such as lovage, sage and oregano, can be kept from one year to the next in their own containers, as long as these are large enough to contain the roots and drain well enough to avoid becoming a solid block of ice during the winter months. (You can find out more about over-wintering perennials in containers in Chapter Six.)

Herbs can also be grown as part of any planting combin- ation, as described back in Chapter Four. The low mat-forming herbs such as thyme and marjoram can become the cascading part of a decorative combination if planted so they can tumble out of a container. And borage, rosemary and sage can help to fill in a floral arrangement with some attractive and fragrant foliage.

So whether you grow them strictly for the kitchen, or as part of your mix of decorative plants, herbs should be part of any container garden.

Planting mixtures for herbs

Herbs have traditionally done well in less-than-perfect soils. In nature, many of them tend to proliferate where other plants have difficulty. Which means that they are very easy for us to grow in containers.

For the most part, the herbs mentioned in the lists in this chapter do best in a well-drained planting mixture. They need a good supply of moisture on hand, but they don't want to sit in damp conditions.

For this reason, the best planting mixture is one with plenty of perlite (or sand) in it, as well as a good loose texture to encourage root growth and aeration. The following planting mix is a good general-purpose one for these herbs.

HERB PLANTING MIX
1 part Potting soil
1 part Compost
1 part Coir/peat
2 parts Perlite
Fertilizer (one handful per three plants)

The fertilizer quantity may seem rather low, but that's on purpose. Many of the herbs that rely on essential oils for their aroma or flavour seem to produce more of them if they are slightly under-fed. If the mixture is too rich, they can turn out lush but less tasty.

CULINARY HERBS

ANNUAL HERBS

Basil
Borage
Chamomile
Chervil
Coriander
Dill
Parsley (a biennial)
Rosemary
Savoury

PERENNIAL HERBS

Chives
Lavender
Lovage
Marjoram
Mint
Oregano
Rosemary
Sage
Tarragon
Thyme

OTHER USEFUL HERBS

ANNUAL

Caraway (stews & baking)
Geranium robertianum / herb Robert (tea)
Lavandula dentata / Spanish lavender (aromatic)
Matricaria recutita / chamomile (tea)
Reseda odorata/ mignonette (potpourris & perfume)
Rumex acidosa / sorrel (salads & soups)

PERENNIAL

Melissa / lemon balm (tea)
Mentha villosa / mojito mint (real mojito flavouring)
Mentha pulegium / pennyroyal (tea)
Nepeta cataria / catnip (need I say more!)
Symphytum / comfrey (tea & green manure)
Ruta graveolens / rue (stews & salads)

Herb varieties

There are literally hundreds of plants that are listed as "herbs" by seed and plant suppliers. They are usually plants whose parts have some use to people for culinary, medicinal, colouring, fragrance or trade purposes.

I have limited the number of "herbs" mentioned in this

chapter to those we use regularly in the kitchen and around the home. They are broken down into annual and perennial varieties, so that people will know which ones need to be replenished each year.

Tomatoes and other big vegetables

Just because you may not have a garden, don't give up on growing your own crops of food plants. You can grow any type of vegetable that you like in the right container.

In this section of this chapter we'll look at growing some of the larger vegetables such as tomatoes, peppers, and the squash and cabbage families. Because they can grow quite large root systems, these big plants should be grown in large deep containers. They should also be given the very best exposure to sun that you have. They will only do well if you can give them a minimum of 4 hours of direct sun every day. Less sun will mean less strong growth and may reduce the harvest you'll get from them.

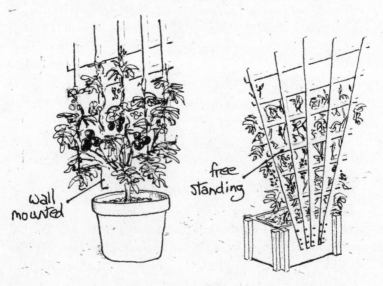

wall mounted

free standing

[FIG. 49] TOMATO TRELLISES

Containers for large vegetables

The larger plants such as tomato and squash vines will need space to grow to their full potential. You can let them sprawl all over the place, but a much better alternative is to train them upwards on supports. Wherever you position your plants, you have to make allowance for this. You can either use a convenient wall or post to fix a trellis or netting against, or you can use a free-standing trellis frame that's connected to the container. Remember that the mature plants can weigh enough to put quite a strain on this support system, so it should be strong enough to be up to the task. [Fig 49]

The more compact plants such as peppers and cabbage can be grown without any extra support, as they will be able to hold up their own growth.

The containers for these large vegetables should be as deep and as large as possible. The large vegetables are heavy feeders, meaning they will need to be able to grow a large volume of roots and have access to a steady supply of food and water. Ideally the containers should be deep so the root system can provide plenty of anchorage for the plant. Fertilizing instructions are given with each crop.

Here is a chart that will give you some idea of the *ideal* container size for various vegetable plants. You can get away with smaller sized containers, but you'll have to feed and water them much more often. For vegetable plants that you don't see listed, use the one that corresponds nearest in size.

PLANT	CONTAINER SIZE
Cabbage, chard	9 litres (2 gallons)
Cucumber (vine)	16 litres (3.5 gallon)
Cucumber (bush)	9 litres (2 gallons)
Pepper (bush)	9 litres (2 gallons)
Squash/melon (vine)	16 litres (3.5 gallons)
Tomato, indeterminate (vine)	22 litres (5 gallons)
Tomato, determinate (bush)	16 litres (3.5 gallons)
Zucchini	9 litres (2 gallons)

Planting mixtures for large vegetables

These larger plants will do best in a fairly heavy planting mixture that contains a high mineral nutrient content, and that is able to hold plenty of water.

For that reason the best mixture will contain a high degree of soil and compost for their mineral nutrients, and some vermiculite to help hold plenty of water. To avoid the mixture becoming soggy, some perlite (or sand) will assist with good drainage.

LARGE VEGETABLE MIX
3 parts Potting soil
3 parts Compost
1 part Perlite
1 part Vermiculite
Fertilizer (one handful per gallon of mixture)

The fertilizer used in the initial mixture should be a slow-release granular organic variety, and it should be well blended into the mixture. For the flowering plants (cuke, tomato, pepper, zucchini) it should be one high in phosphor and potassium, such as 4-7-7. For the leafy plants (cabbage, chard, bok choi) a high nitrogen fertilizer, such as 7-2-2, is essential.

However, starting halfway through the season these large plants will benefit from being fed every two weeks with a liquid fertilizer.

They can also benefit from foliar feeding at any time. Plants are not only able to ingest nutrients through their roots, but they can also absorb them in smaller amounts through their foliage. So if you spray the leaves of a plant with fertilized water, the plant is bound to benefit.

Just mix up a batch of fertilized water, put it in a sprayer and coat the upper surfaces of the leaves. In this way you can quickly give a plant a shot of extra nitrogen or phosphor at any time during the growing period.

This is a great use for "manure tea". To make a batch of manure tea, soak a small sack of manure in a bucket of water overnight. The resulting "tea" should be diluted half-and-half with water before applying to the foliage.

Other vegetable crops

There are several other vegetable types that are quite practical to grow in containers. Perhaps the only one not recommended would be sweet corn! But each of these others may require a different setup when it comes to containers and locations.

One thing they will all need in common is a good exposure to the sun and a consistent supply of water and nutrients.

The optimum planting mixture is one that is not too heavy so that the light roots can penetrate easily. But because each of the following crops is grown for different parts of the plant, the fertilizer needs will vary. Check the fertilizer formula needed for each one carefully, because using the wrong one may reduce the quantity of the harvest.

Peas & beans

Usually these crops are planted from seed, and a large number of them are grown quite close together. So the ideal container for them should be more like a window box than a pot, and it should be at least 20cm (8 inches) deep.

That way you can have a few rows of them growing together with about 15cm (6 inches) between each plant. You will also have to take into consideration the growth habits of particular varieties of peas and beans. Depending on their height at maturity, they will need different types of support.

In the case of bush beans and most peas, they will grow about 90cm (36 inches) high. They will need something to grow up or rest against to that height. You can use branches from trees or shrubs, or you can set up a system of horizontal strings between posts.

Then there are pole beans, which can reach heights of 2 to

2.5 meters (6-8 feet) without any problem. For these you'll need either a wooden frame to support them, or one string per plant to that height, and they will get quite heavy so the string and its support must be sturdy. [Fig 50]

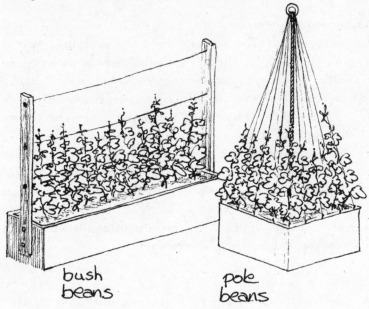

bush beans

pole beans

[FIG. 50] BEAN SUPPORTS

The planting mixture for these crops should be full of minerals and able to stay moist for long periods of time.

The fertilizer can be the same as one used for tomatoes, as the flowering process is important for the harvest, and the added calcium is important too.

PEA & BEAN PLANTING MIXTURE
4 parts Potting soil
2 parts Compost
I part Coir/peat
2 parts Perlite
2 parts Vermiculite

Tomato or flowering plant fertilizer (one handful
   per plant)

Peas are an early crop, traditionally planted in the early spring when it's still quite cool outside. They are usually harvested by the early summer, but there are some longer season varieties available now.

Beans are traditionally planted in late spring or early summer, once the soil has warmed up, but in containers this is not as much of a problem. They are harvested from mid to late summer, with pole bean crops lasting much longer. When crops of peas have finished, you can remove them and use the same container to plant another crop of beans.

Root crops

The most popular of these vegetables are beets, carrots and parsnips. Because they are prized for their long root section, they need to be grown in quite deep containers that are at least

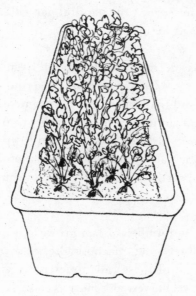

[FIG. 51] RADISHES

20cm (8 inches) deep so that they can reach their full potential.

Radishes, although strictly a root crop, are so small that they can be grown in a much shallower container, or they can be planted in between rows of other root crops. [Fig 51] The planting mixture for root crops should be very loose and crumbly, so the roots have no difficulty in penetrating and spreading. A suitable mixture is very similar to the one given previously for small containers.

The fertilizer should encourage root growth rather than foliage, so it should be high in phosphor (P) such as 0-5-0. You can use bone meal or rock phosphate for this.

ROOT VEGETABLE PLANTING MIXTURE
3 parts Potting soil
1 part Compost
1 part Coir/peat
1 part Perlite
1 part Vermiculite
Phosphate fertilizer (one handful per gallon
   of planting mixture)

These crops are traditionally planted from seed sown very early in the spring. They can be planted in rows about 10cm (4 inches) apart, and then once they've sprouted the tiny plants have to be thinned out until there is only one plant every 5cm (2 inches). This will give the root room to spread to its full width. You can actually pick less mature carrots and beets at an earlier stage and eat them while they are very young and tender.

Leaf crops

There are a large number of fast-growing leaf crops such as lettuce, spinach, arugula, mache, radiccio, sorrel, rocket and the mixture of all of these called mesclun. They are shallow rooted and can be harvested almost as soon as they start producing their leaves.

If you want each plant to grow to its full size, they need to be given space of about 15cm (6 inches) between plants. However, for the mixture of mesclun the seed can be sown quite close together as the crop is harvested by chopping off leaves in sections with a pair of scissors.

Containers for leaf crops can vary, depending on how you want to grow them. If you want to grow single large heads, they can be planted individually in small pots. Or they can be grown in rows close together in a long container such as a window box, that's at least 20cm (8 inches) deep. [Fig 52]

[FIG. 52] LETTUCE IN POTS AND WINDOW BOX

The planting mixture for leaf crops can be similar to one for shallow-rooted annual flowers, with plenty of lightweight components that make it easy for root penetration and water retention.

The fertilizer should be high in nitrogen and low in phosphor and potassium such as 7-2-2, to promote leaf growth over flower or stem production.

LEAF CROP PLANTING MIXTURE
3 parts Potting soil
1 part Compost

1 part Coir/peat
1 part Perlite
1 part Vermiculite
Nitrogen fertilizer (one handful per gallon
    of planting mixture)

Leaf crops can all be grown quickly from seed planted in
the late spring, but if you want to get a head start on the season
you can plant seedlings of each variety grown earlier indoors.
  Once you've harvested one area of leaf crops, you can plant
another crop from seeds or seedlings to follow, keeping this
up throughout the season for a constant harvest of salad greens.

CHAPTER SIX

Special Techniques

Setting up for planting

When you're planning to plant up some containers, I've always found it useful to get everything organized ahead of time to make the job go easier. Once you start the process, it's so much better if you don't have to stop and go hunting for something halfway through.

This is particularly true if you're planting up an arrangement of different annuals into something like a window box. You'll need all of the plant varieties handy, and if you've made some sort of planting plan to follow then that should be accessible too.

It's also a good idea to have an area prepared where you can do this particular job. One thing I hate doing is working on my knees, so I set up a potting table to allow the planting work to be done at a convenient height. You can even set one up temporarily while you pot up your containers, because it will save you a lot of muscle strain. [Fig 54]

Here are some of the things that you might consider gathering onto your potting table before you start.

Containers (cleaned and ready for use)
Planting mixture (either one that's suitable for all of
  your containers, or the various components to make
  different mixtures.)
Fertilizer (organic slow-release granules suited to the
  plants)

Water crystals (to be added as you fill the containers)

Screen sections/pantyhose (to cover holes in the bottom of containers)

Plastic sheet (to waterproof inside of terra cotta containers)

Scoop/trowel (to ladle in planting mixture as you plant)

Knife (to cut plants and roots)

Scissors/shears (for any trimming or pruning)

Old paint brush (to clean leaves and container surfaces)

Watering can (to thoroughly soak each planted container)

Broom (to sweep up planting area afterwards)

[FIG. 54] POTTING TABLE

It's a really good idea to set up your planting area in the shade and out of the sun, for a couple of reasons. First of all you don't want to expose the plants to the heat and drying effects of the sun while you're messing around with them and potentially exposing their roots. And secondly, since transplanting can be a bit of a shock to a plant, once you've planted up your containers it gives the plants some time to get accustomed to their new home before being exposed to strong light.

The majority of your container planting will probably be done quite early in the spring, while the weather is still cool, and this is an advantage for the plants as it reduces the stress on them.

In fact, you can often plant up containers well before you get around to planting up your garden beds. This is because the soil in the beds takes time to warm up and dry out, whereas your containers start off with new planting mixture at a warmer temperature.

Also, containers that are positioned off the ground are not exposed to the same low day and night temperatures as exists at ground level. There can be a difference of several degrees between them. This means that you can often have containers planted up and growing a couple of weeks before the ground is ready for the same plants. In fact containers that are several feet off the ground, for instance on a balcony, can be literally above the effects of a low-lying frost. This gives these containers an edge in starting growth sooner in the spring and lasting longer in the fall.

Planting tips

Far be it from me to tell you the way to plant up your containers, but if you're new to this game or you've always found this part of the job tricky, then perhaps some of these tips may help you out.

Make an estimate of the amount of planting mixture that you'll need to fill your containers, and have all of the ingredients on hand that will make up this amount of planting mixture (e.g. potting soil, compost, peat moss, perlite and fertilizer).

Use a tub or wheelbarrow to stir together the various

ingredients of your planting mixture ahead of time, and make enough to fill most or all of the containers you're planting.

If you're following a planting mixture recipe that calls for a certain number of "parts" of each ingredient, remember that these "parts" can be measured with anything from a shovel to a spoon, as long as you're consistent.

If you plan on using different planting mixtures for different types of plants, I would suggest doing all of the same type first, then blending up a new batch of planting mixture for the different recipe.

Check each container to see that its drainage holes are clear, and then cover each one with a section of screen or pantyhose. A handful of planting mixture will hold it in place.

You can then proceed to the filling and planting part of the operation, as described later for **Annuals, Perennials,** etc.

One word about watering. All of your containers should be really well watered after they have been planted, to settle the plants and the planting mixture. You should soak the container **slowly** so that the water has time to percolate down through all the levels and start running out of the bottom. This may mean adding some water, and then waiting a few minutes while it settles, and then adding some more, etc. However, I would recommend that you move the containers into their ultimate location BEFORE you water them, so they are not as heavy to carry as they will be once wet.

Annuals

The most commonly-planted container plants are annuals. They are usually sold in "packs" or "flats" containing from six to a dozen seedlings. Some of the more expensive ones are sold in individual small pots.

The seedlings in flats should be carefully separated by cutting their roots cleanly with a sharp knife, rather than tearing them apart, as it does less damage to their roots. You can do this either by cutting into the flat and removing them individually (like cutting cake squares out of a pan), or by cutting away the sides of the flat first and then dividing the seedlings with the knife.

Each seedling in a soft skinned pack can usually be removed by turning the pack over and pushing on the base of one section, while simultaneously tugging the seedling out with the other hand. [Fig 55]

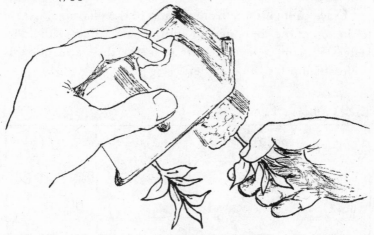

[FIG. 55] REMOVING SEEDLINGS

Fill the container you're working on with enough planting mixture to bring it up to the level where the seedlings and plants can be set in position.

Add the amount of organic fertilizer that you've determined will be needed, and stir it into the planting mixture.

If you are using "water crystals" to help keep the planting mixture moist (see Chapter Three), add the correct amount now and stir them lightly into the planting mixture.

Press the planting mixture lightly to settle it, and add more mixture if necessary.

If you're planting several annuals in an arrangement in a container, I would suggest you first separate or un-pot all of the seedlings that you'll need. Then arrange them, in the container,

119

roughly in the pattern in which you want to plant them. This way you can re-arrange them and make changes **before** you add the rest of the planting mixture.

Then fill in all around the individual plants with the planting mixture, pressing it gently into place and making sure that there are no air pockets left, until you've covered all of the root balls.

Leave enough space from the top of the planting mixture to the top of the container for adding water. There should be at least 2.5cm (one inch) of space for this, and more is preferable for larger containers. [Fig 56]

[FIG. 56] PLANTING ANNUALS

Perennials

If you are buying perennials to add to a container, they will most likely be sold in individual pots. If you're taking them from your own garden you can divide them from existing plants.

Either way, it's best to have the container and planting mixture all ready so that the plants don't sit around with their roots exposed while you organize things.

Preparing the container with planting mixture, fertilizer and other additions such as water crystals can be done in the same way as mentioned before for **Annuals.**

Once you have the container filled to the planting level, position the perennials until you are satisfied with their

120

arrangement and then fill in around them with planting mixture, leaving space at the top for watering.

Summer bulbs

For the bulbs of summer-blooming plants such as begonia, caladium, canna lily and dahlia you should plant them as early in the spring as possible. To achieve this you have two options.

One way is to bring the containers indoors about a month before you can safely leave them outside, fill them with planting mixture and plant the bulbs directly into them. The bulbs will sprout and start to grow foliage after a couple of weeks, at which point they will need to be put into the best light conditions possible. As soon as the weather warms up enough, you can take the planted containers outside.

Or, if your containers are too large to conveniently move in and out, you can plant the summer bulbs in smaller containers indoors. This should also be done about a month before taking them outside. Once the plants have sprouted and grown, and the weather improves, you can take them outdoors and transplant the bulbs into your larger containers.

Both of these methods will give the summer bulbs a head start on the season, with a much better chance of them flowering early and lasting longer.

Summer bulbs tend to flower later in the season, so they are often planted in containers in conjunction with constantly-blooming annuals. This provides a display in the earlier part of the season until the summer bulbs are ready to bloom.

These summer bulbs require a few different planting methods, but they break down into about four different ones.

Begonia, cyclamen and nerine The tubers should be planted so that their tops are just visible above the planting mixture. Care should be taken when watering not to get the surface of the tubers too wet.

Dahlia The tuber needs to be planted at a 45 degree angle, with the stem end uppermost, and the whole thing buried beneath the planting mixture. Depending on the exact variety and how tall the stems get, you may need to provide stakes to keep them secure.

Gloriosa daisy The tubers should be planted in their container and covered with a final 5cm (2 inches) of planting mixture. As the vines emerge, they will need support to reach a trellis or netting so that they can grow up to 2.5 meters (8 feet) during the season.

All the rest (achimenes, agapanthus, allium {many}, caladium, canna lily, liatris, lilium {many}, oxalis, ranunculus {many}) These bulbs and corms and tubers can be planted so they are well buried in planting mixture. The larger "bulbs" such as agapanthus, canna lily and lillium should be buried about 10cm (4 inches) beneath the surface, and all the smaller ones can be buried about 5cm (2 inches). [Fig 57]

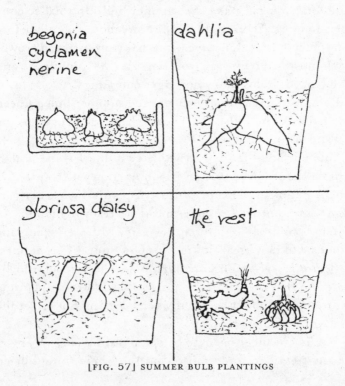

[FIG. 57] SUMMER BULB PLANTINGS

Spring bulbs

The bulbs of spring blooming plants should be planted in the early autumn, at the same time as they are normally planted into garden beds. It's recommended that you **don't** plant these bulbs in terra cotta or porous containers, as they will absorb moisture which will then expand when it freezes and damage the material of the container.

The larger bulbs such as allium, daffodil and tulip should be planted in the container so that the base of each bulb is 18cm (7 inches) from the surface. The space between each bulb should be about the diameter of the bulb.

Smaller bulbs like crocus, chionodoxa, galanthus and scilla should be planted at a depth of 12cm (5 inches).

If you want to, you can plant a layer of large bulbs first and then a layer of smaller ones above them, all in the same container. That way you'll have a double blooming as the small ones bloom first, followed by the larger ones. [Fig 58]

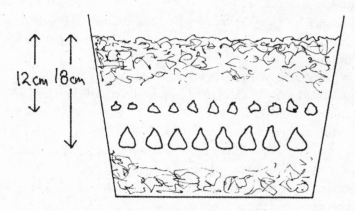

[FIG. 58] 2-LAYER SPRING BULB PLANTING

Once they are planted, the containers of spring bulbs can stay outdoors over the winter. In locations where mid-winter temperatures fall below freezing the containers must be protected either by being partially buried in the garden, or else covered with lots of snow for the duration of the winter.

123

In the late winter and early spring, the containers can be lifted into sunny locations to warm up and start blooming.

Once the bulbs have bloomed, they can be removed from the containers, so that you can re-use the containers for something else. Unless you're able to re-plant the finished bulbs into the soil of the garden to keep growing over the summer, I would suggest throwing them on the compost because they won't perform well again.

Shrubs

As long as the plant and the container are suitable for each other, there's no reason why you can't grow almost any type of shrub in a pot or planter. The suitability I'm referring to has more to do with size to accommodate all of the roots over a period of years than anything else.

Often when we buy shrubs at a garden centre, they are in medium-sized "selling pots" all ready to plant. But when choosing a container to put the shrub into, you have to take into consideration the mature size of the shrub. The ultimate spread and height of the plant will have a big effect on the size of the root ball that will grow along with it.

Conversely, if the size of the root ball is restricted by a container that's too small, the upper growth of the plant may be stunted or adversely affected.

Ideally, a container for a shrub should be as wide as the spread of the plant. If it's a bit narrower, then the container should be a bit deeper to make up for it.

Planting shrubs into containers is not difficult, as long as you remember a couple of basic rules.

The most important rule is to plant each shrub at **exactly** the same height that it was in its packaging when you bought it. You want the soil level to remain the same, no deeper and no shallower. You don't want to bury more of the stem length than they way it was growing before, and you don't want to expose any of the root ball. [Fig 59]

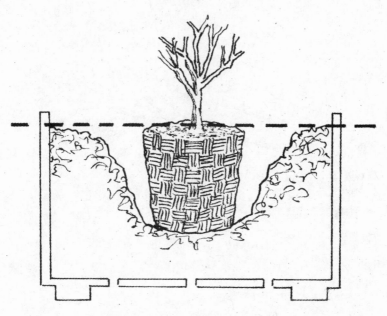

[FIG. 59] SHRUB PLANTING

The other important rule is to check the root system when you turn the shrub out of its selling pot. You may find that there are roots growing in circles all around the outer surface of the root ball. These can actually choke the plant's growth if left that way. To avoid this, take a sharp knife and slice the root ball with several vertical slits, about 5cm (2 inches) deep and spaced about 10cm (4 inches) apart. This will encourage new root growth outwards into the planting mixture once the shrub has been planted. [Fig 60]

The best way to plant a shrub that you've bought in a selling pot is to partly fill the container with planting mixture, and then position the shrub *in its selling pot* and fill in around it with more mixture. Then when you lift out the shrub along with its pot it will leave a perfectly-sized hole at the right depth. You then remove the shrub from its selling pot, and re-insert the root ball into the hole in the container. Pack the planting mixture in around the root ball, and adjust the height of the

125

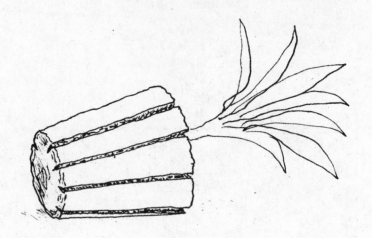

[FIG. 60 CUTTING ROOT BALL

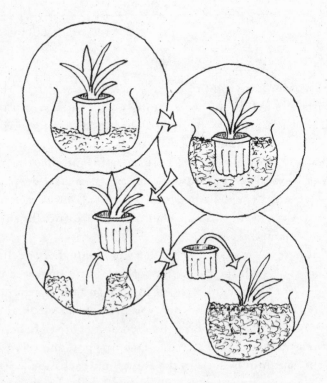

[FIG. 61 PLANTING POTTED SHRUB

planting mixture if necessary. [Fig 61]

If the shrub is sold with bare roots, you should soak the roots in a bucket of water overnight to soften them. Then spread the roots out as much as possible and hold the whole plant over the container, with the roots in place, and gradually fill the container with planting mixture, packing it carefully into place around the roots. This technique works well for roses that are sold in a narrow bag with bare roots inside. [Fig 62]

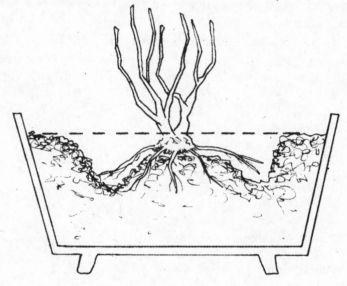

[FIG. 62] PLANTING BARE-ROOTED PLANTS

There are three types of shrubs that are fun to have in containers; deciduous, evergreen and tender shrubs.

Deciduous shrubs These will lose their leaves each autumn, but they often grow faster than evergreens and provide lots of potential for a container garden.

Deciduous plants can be pruned quite extensively to create particular shapes or growth habits. Keeping the tips of their branches trimmed will make them fill out and become more compact, whereas letting them grow un-pruned will allow a

127

more natural shape. Many deciduous shrubs provide blooms, most often in the spring and early summer, while others are attractive because of their variegated or strongly coloured foliage.

Non-flowering shrubs should be pruned in the late winter or early spring to guide the shape they will grow during the season.

Flowering shrubs should be pruned just after they have flowered, by removing their faded blooms and trimming any foliage necessary.

Here are some deciduous shrubs that are suitable for container growing. Those that flower in the spring are marked (SF), those in the summer (SUF).

Abutilon (SF)
Berberis thunbergii
Calluna (SF)
Cephalanthus (SF)
Comptonia
Cornus alba
Datura (SUF)
Euonymus alatus
Forsythia (SF)
Genista (SF)
Hydrangea (SUF)
Paeonia (SF)
Persicaria (SUF)
Potentilla fruticosa (SF)
Ricinus (SUF)
Rose (SUF)
Ruta graveolens
Spirea bumalda (SUF)
Sorbaria (SUF)
Stephanandra (SF)
Viburnum trilobum (SF)
Weigela (SF)

EVERGREEN SHRUBS	
BROAD-LEAVED	CONIFEROUS
Buxus (Box)	Abies dwarf
Cotoneaster	Chamaecyparis
Euonymous fortunei	Juniperus dwarf
Ilex (Holly)	Picea dwarf
Rhododendron	Pinus dwarf
& azalea hybrids	Thuja dwarf
Yucca	

Evergreen shrubs These keep their foliage all year long, and there are two types. The broad-leaved evergreens and the confiers (with needle-like leaves).

A couple of broad-leaved evergreens produce flowers. The *ilex* (holly) has insignificant flowers that lead to bright red fruit, as long as you have both male and female plants. And the *azalea* and *rhododendron* both produce showy flowers in the early spring.

Evergreens are slower-growing than deciduous, but a certain amount of pruning will guide their shape. They can be kept small and compact by cutting off the tip of the uppermost branch (the "leader"), or encouraged to grow tall and narrow by trimming back the side growth.

Tender shrubs These are plants that are not tough enough to withstand temperatures below zero, as they come from warm temperate or tropical regions. They can spend the spring and summer outdoors, but they must be brought indoors for the late autumn and winter months if the temperatures plunge.

These plants are grown for their blooms, but they flower at different times of the season. Frequent deadheading will encourage new blooms to form on most of them. Pruning times are different for each of them, and the details are noted below.

Potted azalea, prune after spring flowering
Camellia, prune after spring flowering
Citrus, prune in the spring

Gardenia jasminoides, prune after flowering
Hibiscus, prune in autumn
Nerium oleander, prune in autumn

Pruning and grooming tips

One of the secrets to good plant growth is to be able to use a pair of pruning shears in ways that help to train and care for the plant.

Pruning directs the way in which a plant grows, and can often actually encourage better growth than if the plant were left to its own devices. Grooming helps to keep the plant healthy by removing unwanted or ineffective growth.

When you're pruning or cutting off foliage from a stem, there's definitely a right way to do it. You should always cut just **above** a node, as close as possible without actually touching the node. This node, or junction, is where the new growth will come from so you don't want to damage it. Also, if you leave any uncut length of stem above the node it will die back anyway, and it might even become infected which is not what you want. So make your cuts close to the node, and as clean a cut as possible. [Fig 63]

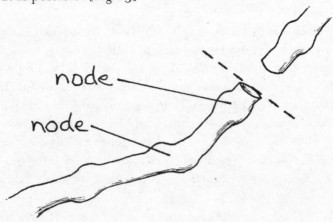

[FIG. 63] PRUNING ABOVE NODE

Let's start with the two most basic pruning techniques for any plant; tip pruning and side pruning.

Tip pruning means literally to cut off the growing tip of a branch or stem. It's often referred to as "pinching". This immediately stops the further upward growth of the stem. As a result, since the plant wants to keep growing, you will force new growth to sprout from nodes in the stem **below** where you cut. The end result is that the stem doesn't get any longer, but it starts to fill out sideways. This technique is used to encourage denser and more compact growth.

For example, if you cut the tips off a dahlia in the early part of the season, you'll produce a plant that has more side shoots. It will be a shorter and more compact plant. The larger number of side shoots will produce more flowers, but they will be slightly smaller than if you left the single stem to grow.

Tip pruning is frequently done to make plants grow with more foliage or more flowers, to force a single stem to fill out as much as possible rather than just growing long. It's probably the most widely used form of pruning, because it has the most impact on making plants look full and robust.

Side pruning means just the opposite. If you trim off any side stems when you see them sprout you'll force all the plant's energy into the main stem.

In the example of the dahlia, side pruning will give you a much taller plant and the single flower head will be much larger.

Side pruning is less often practiced, unless you're trying to grow an enormous prize-winning dahlia bloom, or you want stems and branches to grow as long as possible.

Obviously, with both of these techniques you'll probably be pruning or pinching off many stems or branches on the same plant, not just one. This will increase the effect of the pruning operation, as the plant will grow into the shape that you're encouraging.

Unwanted growth is another common reason for pruning.

In particular, this would mean removing stems or branches that fall into the categories of "The Three D's"; dead, damaged or diseased.

Dead parts are fairly obvious, as they usually result from broken or badly bent stems. When growth stops and a section of stem dies, it's never going to come back to life again so you may as well remove it ASAP. This will speed up the process of new growth starting below where the break was.

Damaged stems are very similar. If a bent stem is affecting the circulation within the plant, it should be trimmed off like a dead one. If a pair of crossed stems is rubbing against each other and causing surface skin loss, one of them should be removed before they both get damaged beyond repair.

Diseased stems or foliage should be removed if they are going to adversely affect the rest of the plant. You can treat certain diseases such as mildews to stop them from spreading without having to remove the foliage. But other diseases, such as blight, that might spread should be dealt with by removal.

Grooming a plant is something where you have to use a bit of common sense rather than hard and fast rules. Most of the time it involves trimming off some excess leaves to let more light into things underneath. Or removing a whole stem that's growing in the wrong direction or getting in the way.

I would also mention the most basic grooming technique of all, and that's called "deadheading".

Deadheading refers to removing the spent or dead heads of flowers once they have finished blooming. It's not just a cosmetic thing, although there's nothing wrong with keeping a plant looking neat. Deadheading can actually encourage a flowering plant to produce more blooms.

If you leave the flower heads on a plant once they've finished, each one will try to set seeds. This actually reduces the vigour of the plant because the plant figures that its job of continuing the species is done. Whereas if you keep deadheading the old flowers and never let them go to seed, the plant has the inclination to keep producing more new buds and blooms. It's a way of keeping a plant looking neat as well as keeping it vigorous.

There are some plants like impatiens and small begonias that self-deadhead quite well, dropping their flowers without setting seeds. But the vast majority of flowers will benefit from this regular grooming exercise.

Using vertical space

Very often with container gardening you're dealing with places that have limited space, such as decks and balconies. Under these circumstances, you should always try and make use of the vertical dimension to add to your space. This can mean encouraging things grow upwards, or letting them cascade downwards.

Upwards growth can have several advantages. It can be used as a screen to shelter or protect you, or to cut out an unwanted view. It can also get plants up into an area where there is more light, thereby giving them a new lease on life and a chance at better growth.

Plants that grow well upwards will still need a helping hand along the way. To start with, they will need to be guided from the container onto whatever support you have provided. And then as they grow, they may need a bit of training to guide them from one place to another. They can also be prompted to grow many more stems if you pinch the growing tips quite early in the season, forcing them to produce several side stems instead of just one main stem.

Some plants like *clematis* and *lathyrus* (sweet pea) throw out short tendrils that grab and twist onto the support to hold their weight. Others like *parthenocissus* (Virginia creeper) use small suckers on the end of their tendrils to hold fast to walls and supports. But the majority of climbers like *ipomoea* (morning glory) and *wisteria* get up there by twisting themselves around whatever support they can find.[Fig 64]

Which brings me to the types of supports that vertical plants need in order to perform properly. Much of the decision as to what to use has to be based on the ultimate size, and therefore weight, of the plant. An annual patch of *mandevilla* may be able to get by with a simple arrangement of strings. But perennial such as *hydrangea* or *vitis* are going to need quite a permanent and robust frame.

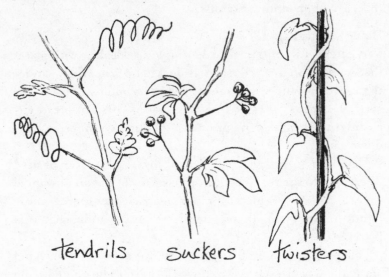

tendrils   suckers   twisters

[FIG. 64] THREE TYPES OF CLIMBERS

Lightweight annuals can be trained up lengths of twine, which have to be supported at the top by nails or hooks. There are special nails that work well in brick and mortar situations. These methods allow each stem or group of stems to twist their way around one single string, leaving rather separate columns of plants.

A better way might be to use lightweight netting that's supported in various places by wall nails or strong staples in wood. The individual stems can then spread sideways as well as upwards giving you more coverage and spreading the weight a bit. And the netting is almost invisible, so you see the plants and not the supports.

But remember that even so-called "lightweight" annuals will end up the season with a substantial weight, particularly when wet from rain. The nails or hooks for your supports will have to be very solidly embedded to take the strain.

Heavier plants will need something much more substantial than string, particularly if they are perennial and will be in place for several years. You can spread netting over a frame of wood for a lighter-looking system. But for real strength you should make a framework of strong wood that can last for several years. There are ready-made trellises that can be used singly or in combination with each other, or you can make your own system with thin lumber and screws. Just remember that the gaps between sections should not be so large that the plant can't reach to twine around them.

Downwards growth is the easiest to manage, because you're just letting gravity do the work. Plants that would normally climb upwards can be allowed just to trail downwards without any particular support. However, many of these plants can grow several feet in one season, so they are not always the best candidates for using as cascading plants as they can get out of hand.

But there are a few particular annual plants that are used specifically because of their trailing habit, which quickly tumble over the sides of a container and grow less than a meter (3 feet) during the growing season.

The best-known foliage plants are *dichondra, helichrysum, iresine, senecio mikanioides* (German ivy), *solanum jasminoides* (star of Jerusalem), *vinca major* and herbs such as *marjoram, oreganum* and *thymus*.

Those that cascade well with flowers are *alyssum, asarina, bacopa, begonia, diascia, fuchsia, lobelia, mesembryanthemum, gypsophila, nemisia, nierembergia, pelargonium peltatum* (ivy-leafed geranium), various *petunia* varieties, *tropaeolum* (nasturtium) and *verbena*.

To make sure that your cascading plants stay compact and look nice and full, you should pinch the growing tips quite soon after they've been planted. This will force them to grow numerous side shoots before they start growing longer, and it will ensure that the upper part of the plant will fill the container before it spills over the edge to grow downwards.

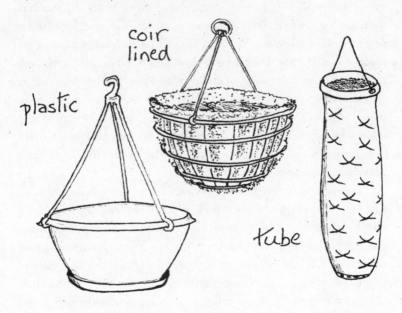

[FIG. 65] HANGING BASKETS

Hanging baskets

Another popular way of taking advantage of the cascading properties of plants is to put them in hanging baskets. There are several different styles of hanging containers that are worth mentioning.

The *open pot* with wire or plastic arms for support is simply a pot filled with planting mixture and plants.

The *wire basket* is a framework of strong wires, lined with sphagnum moss or coir to support the soil inside. Large wire baskets can even have small plants inserted in their sides, to create a ball-like effect of blooms.

The *plant tube* is a relatively new concept, where a cylinder of plastic film, sealed at the bottom, is filled with planting mixture and then plants are inserted through slits in the plastic all around to create a column of flowers. [Fig 65]

All these hanging baskets require frequent attention to their water needs, as they are hanging exposed to wind and perhaps sun that will dry them out quickly. Make sure that wherever you hang them, they are easily accessible with a watering can or hose. They can also be hung with a rope-and-pulley system so they can be lowered for watering purposes.

Hanging baskets should be filled with a lighter-weight planting mixture, to reduce the stress on the hangers. There is a suggested mixture for this at the end of Chapter Two.

End of season cleanup

For the same reason that containers can be started slightly earlier in the springtime, they can also last a bit longer in the autumn than your ground-level planting beds. Containers that are off the ground are less susceptible to early frosts, and will often last well into the cooler part of the autumn.

But eventually, all good things must come to an end, and you'll have to put your container garden to bed for the winter. You can do this in much the way as you would for your regular garden.

The annuals can be pulled out of the containers and chopped up for the compost pile. The perennials can be cut back to leave a few short stems above the planting mixture, and the cut sections added to the compost. The same use can be made of the leaves from any deciduous shrubs you have in containers.

Both deciduous and evergreen shrubs should be protected for the winter, if needed. The simplest form of protection is to wrap garden twine around the branches from bottom to top, to help support the branches in case they get loaded with any heavy wet snow weighing them down. If they're exposed to severe winter winds, you may also want to wrap them with burlap or winter-wrap fabric to protect the foliage of evergreens and the branches of deciduous plants such as roses.

The containers themselves also require some care for the winter.

First of all, any terra cotta or porous containers that had annuals in them should be emptied of planting mixture and taken indoors so they are not exposed to freezing temperatures. If they freeze, any moisture that's soaked into the material of the container will expand, and this can crack or shatter them.

For other containers that had annuals in them, you have a choice. The planting mixture from small pots can be tipped out and mixed into the compost. But the larger containers don't really need to be emptied completely. My Scottish nature tells me not to dump all of that wonderful planting mixture every season, only to have to replace it the very next year. So what I do is to remove about half of the planting mixture from the larger containers and mix it in the compost. The rest I leave in the container, and even as it freezes and expands upwards it won't hurt the container. Then next spring all I have to do is add *half* as much planting mixture, stir it together with what was left over, and I'm ready to plant.

For containers that have perennials or shrubs in them, there's not much you need to do to them. You can remove any weeds you see growing, and then top dress the planting mixture with a layer of compost.

Over-wintering plants outdoors

Hardy perennials and shrubs can normally spend the winter outdoors in the ground without any risk. That's because they have root systems and storage organs that can tolerate the below-zero temperatures, and the soil protects them from severe damage.

However, if you want to leave your perennials and shrubs outdoors in containers over the winter, there are a few things to consider.

First of all, perennials and shrubs that are only marginally hardy in your zone will probably have a tough time staying alive in a container over the winter. They should be taken out of the container and plunged into a spot in an empty garden bed, then dug up and re-potted in the spring.

Secondly, even hardy perennials and shrubs need some precautions during the winter. The soil should stay hard **all** winter, even if there's a mid-winter thaw. To achieve this you should mulch the surface of the planting mixture, and pile up as much snow over the containers as possible for the duration of the winter. You can always uncover them in the spring, but the snow is the best insulator available, and it's free! Also the container must drain really well, as you don't want autumn's rain to flood the planting mixture and freeze into a popsicle.

There are ways to actually winterize your containers, but they have to be done before you plant them. The idea is to line the sides and base with panels of foam insulation, just like you would when building a house to insulate the walls. A single 7.5cm (1.5 inch) layer is sufficient, but you have to make sure that there are holes in the bottom panel that line up with the drain holes of the container.

Even with these precautions, you may lose the occasional plant over the winter because its root system just couldn't take the extreme cold, or the damp caused the root crown to split and get diseased. The larger the container, the lower the risk of damage from freezing. I've found that pushing a bunch of containers together into a sheltered location, and making sure they get covered with a blanket of snow as soon as possible in the early part of the winter is the best guarantee of keeping them all safe.

Over-wintering plants indoors
An alternative for less hardy plants that you want to keep until next spring is to bring them indoors for the winter. Obviously you have to have the space to do this, but there are a few different ways to keep plants going from one season to the next.

Sunny window.
For plants that are expensive to buy every year, like the *pelar-*

gonium varieties that are very popular, you can keep the whole plant growing as if it were a flowering houseplant. All you need is a very sunny window.

The plant should be in its own pot, and kept in a place that gets as much direct sunlight as possible every day. During the depths of winter, with short days and cloudy weather, this can be tough to do but if you've got the place you can manage.

You'll find that the plant tends to grow longer and thinner than it would outdoors in the summer, but you can overcome this by pinching the growing tips often (to slow its lengthy growth) or by cutting it back in length a couple of times during the winter. If you just let it grow you'll probably end up with a very long version of the plant, with stems that may break under the weight of this extra length, so keeping it short is important.

Once the days start to lengthen in March, you can allow the plant to start putting on some growth, and you can feed it as well. It may even begin flowering for you. By the late spring it will be ready to be used outdoors again.

Artificial lights.

In much the same way as keeping them in a sunny window, you can keep plants growing under artificial lights. With the greater amount of light and longer day length that you can give them this way, your plants will actually grow in a very healthy and convincing way. The more light you give them, the more compact they will grow, and the more likely it is that they will flower for you all of the time.

You may need to cut them back during the winter months if they grow too tall, but they will be far less thin and lanky than the plants described before that are kept only in a sunny window.

The least expensive and most efficient type of lights to do this with are regular fluorescent lamps. The ideal setup uses the common 120cm (4 foot) fixture with two or four lamps in it. The lamps are 40 or 32 watts each in power, and you should

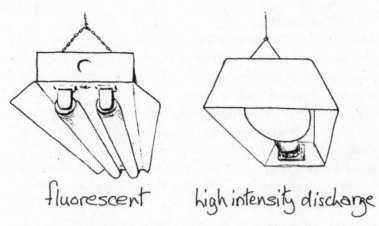

fluorescent   high intensity discharge

[FIG. 66] ARTIFICIAL LIGHT SOURCES

buy the Cool White colour as it's the least expensive and perfectly good for the plants. A system this size will look after a
tabletop about 120 by 60cm (4 by 2 feet) covered with plants.

You can buy all the parts from a hardware store for under
$100, or buy a finished kit for double that price. Fluorescent
lamps give off very little heat (in comparison to incandescent
bulbs) so there is no risk of them burning the plant foliage. If
you put them on a timer, set for 18 hours on and 6 hours off,
you'll get the most growth out of your plants.

Even more efficient, but much more expensive, are the
High Intensity Discharge fixtures (HID). These use metal
halide or high-pressure sodium lamps that have an output
anywhere from 250 to 1000 watts, and because of their power
they can grow a small room full of plants in almost high-noon
daylight conditions. But they are a bit large for most home
gardeners, unless you're planning to grow full-sized tomato
plants.

One thing you should **not** use for growing flowering plants
over the winter is the standard incandescent bulb. These give
off far too much heat, and by the time you've moved it far
enough away from the plant to be safe, its light output has
dwindled to a useless amount.

Taking cuttings.

Another way of keeping plants alive from one season to the next is to take several cuttings from the "mother" plant that you like, and grow them over the winter as new plants. You'll need to have either the very sunny window or the artificial lights to do this properly, as the cuttings need as much light as they can get in their growth stages. You can either take the cuttings from an outdoor plant late in the simmer, or from a plant that you are trying to keep over the winter when you trim it back.

The best cuttings to use for this purpose are "tip" cuttings, taken from the growing tip of each stem of the plant. These cuttings can actually be the pieces that you cut off if you're trying to keep the plant compact, as mentioned in the preceding section.

Here's my method for taking and growing cuttings that seems to work for me most of the time. I have about a 95% success rate overall, and I always take a few more cuttings than I really need just in case something goes wrong.

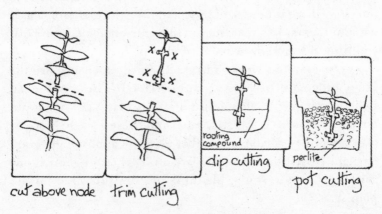

[FIG. 67] TAKING A CUTTING

From the growing tip of a plant cut a 7.5-10cm (3-4 inch) section, cutting just **above** a leaf node so that you don't leave much stem on the plant to die back. From the cutting, trim off all the leaves except the two newest at the very tip. Also, cut the stem cleanly just **below** the lowest leaf node, as this is where the roots will grow from eventually. This trimmed and cut section is now "the cutting", and is ready to grow roots.

Take the cutting and dip the cut end in rooting hormone powder or liquid. (The one exception to this rule that I've found seems to be *pelargonium* cuttings. They work better with no hormone.) Then push the cutting gently into dry perlite in a small pot or cell pack, until it's half buried. Water the pot, and put the potted cutting in the light. Keep the perlite moist at all times.

Within a week or two, roots will grow from the buried node. You can tell that this has happened in a couple of ways. The cutting will start to grow leaves, and it will resist being pulled upwards if you tug it gently. Give it another week to grow a few more roots, then transplant the cutting into a small pot filled with the lightweight planting mixture mentioned in Chapter Two.

From this point onwards, your rooted cutting will continue to grow if you give it lots of light, water it regularly and feed it once a month. It may even start to flower for you at quite an early age. By the time you're ready to plant outdoors, your cutting will be at least as large as the ones you buy each spring at the garden centres and markets. Think of the money you'll save! And you will continue to have examples of the "mother" plant that you took the cutting from in the first place.

Dry storage.

One last method of keeping plants over the winter is rather risky, and only seems to work for the *pelargonium* which is a half-hardy perennial anyway. This method relies on storing the plant "dry" over the winter, and then reviving it again next spring. It's not foolproof, and you may have some losses doing it, but it's a method that can be used by people who have no opportunity to keep the plants growing alive all winter.

At the end of the growing season, cut back nearly all of the growth until the stems are only about 7.5cm (3 inches) long. Bring the potted plant indoors and allow the planting mixture to dry out completely for a couple of weeks. Then turn the pot upside down and remove the plant from the planting mixture. Allow it to dry even more, and then clean off all of the planting mixture until the roots are completely bare.

The roots should now be stored for the winter. You can put them in a paper bag or hang them up, but they must stay completely dry all winter. Then in March, soak the roots overnight in water, and the next day re-pot them in moist planting mixture and expose them to good light conditions. The roots that survived will revive, and start to sprout new stems. All you have to do from then on is treat the new plant as you would any other.

Gardening with disabilities

Growing things in containers can also be a very useful way for people with various disabilities to garden. Anyone with limited mobility, sight or dexterity will find that containers can make it much easier to enjoy the gardening experience.

For a start, containers or raised garden beds can allow people in chairs to work at a convenient height. There's no need to be bending over to work soil at ground level. This elevated gardening method also brings the plants to a level where they can be seen, smelled and touched more easily.

Gardening in containers also reduces a lot of the unnecessary workload. Well-mulched containers seldom need weeding or cultivating, and a good irrigation system removes the chores of constant watering. Also, since the planting mixture is never walked upon, it seldom if ever requires digging to relieve compaction.

The type of containers used for gardeners with disabilities depends to great degree upon the type of disability. For those in chairs or with restricted mobility, tall planters or raised tabletop beds allow almost any decorative or food plants to be grown. For those with limited dexterity, narrow window box style planters allow a large variety of things to be grown, without the need for reaching great distances. Anyone with limited vision can probably manage with a variety of container shapes and sizes, as long as they are securely anchored and free of dangerous surfaces. And for anyone who lives with supervisory assistance, the potential and the pleasures of container gardening is almost unlimited.

There's no reason to stop gardening just because you can't stick a spade in the ground. Containers make all sorts of gardening accessible to people who might otherwise give up a previously enjoyed hobby. And for those who are new to gardening, the pots and planters of container gardening can open up a whole new world.

Problem Solving

You may find that growing things in containers actually produces fewer plant problems for you than growing in garden beds. Containers allow for a very controlled environment, where you get to dictate the exact planting mixture and things like the location of the container. If the plants are cared for properly, they will stay healthy and free of pests.

Weather can have less of an effect on containers too, as you're often able to move a group of plants away from problem situations. You can extend the whole growing season both at the beginning and at the end by protecting against unpredictable frosts at the start and finish of the season. And ground level problems like floods become a thing of the past.

But there are still likely to be a few instances where problems arise. This chapter will try and help you plan for them, and solve them.

Plant problems

By using carefully blended planting mixtures and being up from the ground level, you actually remove many of the soil-borne situations that can lead to problems.

For instance, you should never have to deal with poor drainage or polluted soil because you've had full control over the ingredients of planting mixture.

But there are situations that could arise that require your intervention. If you know about them ahead of time, you may be able to avoid them altogether.

Sparse growth. If you notice that all the plants in a container are doing badly and struggling to grow, this usually comes about from really poor nutrition or very bad drainage.

Check the planting mixture first to see if it's soggy, particularly after a rainstorm. If it is, this may be because the drain hole is blocked with roots or other debris. You'll have to work from underneath with a sharp spike to unblock the drain holes. The only other reason would be because you've blended a very heavy planting mixture full of clay, and the plants are not enjoying it.

If the container is draining well, and the poor growth is happening towards the latter part of the season, perhaps it's because your plants are lacking nutrition. You should have mixed some slow-release organic fertilizer into the original planting mixture, to give the plants the nutrients they need for the first several weeks. Then from July onwards, you should be feeding the plants every couple of weeks with a water-soluble organic fertilizer in your watering can. (See Chapter Three)

Excessive growth. If some of the plants in a container are being choked by other plants, this can be a problem. There are some plants that grow faster than others, and can spread their foliage to the point that they smother their neighbours.

You can either remove the plants that are being choked, or cut back the ones that are getting out of hand. Sometimes by removing a few short stems or some foliage from one plant, you give the suffering plants just enough of a break that they can come back and hold their own. But you should keep an eye on the situation throughout the season, because the fast-growing plant is probably not going to slow down!

If the situation is likely to persist, you may want to consider severely pruning the faster plant to restrict its growth considerably. Remove a lot of the side stems right where they come out of the planting mixture. But for heaven's sake don't prune the growing tips off any long stems because that will just make it spread even more.

Plants fade away. Sometimes some plants in a container just seem to fade away. Their leaves and stems turn brown and they shrivel up completely.

This can often be as a result of the problem mentioned before, of being crowded out and smothered. But it can also happen that a very shallow-rooted plant dries out just a bit too much or once too often, and that's the end of it. I've seen this happen to young *lobelia* plants in the early part of the summer. They don't grow as quickly as their neighbours, they get covered a bit, and then one occasion where the surface of the planting mix dried out too much and they're gone.

A few things can help too avoid this. Plant all of your young plants as deeply as possible, to make sure their roots are well covered. Mulch the exposed surface of the planting mixture to make sure it never dries out. And don't let smaller plants get elbowed out of the light by bigger plants.

Weather damage. Some container plants, particularly when they're young, can get knocked around by the weather to the point of being damaged.

I'm thinking particularly of heavy rain or hail hitting plants with bigger leaves such as *petunia* or *pelargonium*. If they get knocked over just after being planted, this disturbs the fragile feeder roots that are just beginning to grow and the plant may not get over it for quite a while. And I've seen leaves almost stripped off small seedlings by a very heavy rain, and that's not good for it either.

The only way to protect them from this sort of abuse is to be aware that they may need some sort of temporary covering for the first week in their new homes if a storm is predicted. An upturned cardboard box or a sheet of plastic may be all that's needed for a little temporary protection.

Much more long-term and perhaps more insidious is the damage that can be wrought by the wind. Certainly tall plants can be pushed over by a heavy windstorm, and that's easy to see and protect against with some simple stakes.

But it's the relentless daily passage of wind through a gap or across a balcony that can have effects on plants that are difficult to notice right away. All of a sudden you realize that a bunch of plants are looking a bit bedraggled or weak, and there's no obvious reason.

That's because the wind has been constantly blowing by them, sucking the moisture out of the planting mixture and out of the leaves. The plants struggle to keep up the water circulation, but it's a battle they can eventually lose. Or the wind has been twisting and moving the stems and foliage so much that the plants suffer eventual damage.

The only answer to this situation is to be aware right from the start that you may have a wind problem with a part of your growing area. If it's **always** windy in one section, you either have to avoid putting plants there, or perhaps you could erect a section of lattice to act as a windscreen to reduce the strength of the wind.

Plants that are low-growing and with smaller foliage are less susceptible to the wind than tall large-leaved ones. Mulching the surface of the planting mixture always helps to reduce the water loss from the wind. And don't put up any hanging baskets on a windy corner.

Watering problems

As I've mentioned repeatedly in this book, the major problem for containers is having a consistent and adequate water supply. Everything conspires to use up the water in a container, from the weather to the plants themselves. So watering in itself is a problem that I've dealt with in Chapter Three in great detail.

I've just mentioned the drying effects of the wind on plants and planting mixtures, particularly on plants in hanging baskets. And in discussing containers in Chapter One, we looked at the way porous containers such as terra cotta pots dry out so quickly, unless they're protected.

But apart from the actual supply of water, there are a couple of problems that relate to the way water is applied or how it flows in a container.

Down the sides

Let's start with the trickiest one of all. I call it the "side sneak". Picture a pot, made of any material, with a root ball that has dried out a bit too much. This may be because the plants have drunk it dry, or the weather has evaporated it all. So the root ball has shrunk slightly, and all around the edge of the planting mixture, where it normally meets the wall of the pot, there's a little gap.

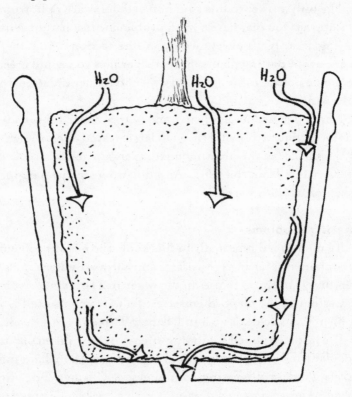

[FIG. 68] SIDE SNEAK WATERING

Then you come along with the watering can and pour in some water from the top. The water runs towards the walls of the pot, and sneaks down the gap at the edge of the planting mixture. It flows downwards and starts oozing out of the drain holes in the bottom of the pot. You see this, and stop watering because you think the root ball is saturated.

You couldn't be further from the truth. In fact NONE of the water penetrated the planting mixture at all, and the root ball is as dry as it was before. All the water snuck down the sides and out of the bottom.

To avoid this you can do several things.

If you see a slight gap around the edges of the root ball, use your finger to push some planting mixture over to plug it, even if it's just at the surface. This will stop the water sneaking away.

If you can lift the container, dunk it in a bucket or tub of water and let it sit there for 15 minutes while it thoroughly absorbs a load of water into its root ball.

And finally, if you cover the surface of the planting mixture with mulch, the gap may never appear, because the planting mixture will probably stay moist for much longer.

Slow to drain

The other big problem with watering containers is quite the opposite. It's when you start pouring water into a pot, and it just sits there. It doesn't drain away, it doesn't soak into the panting mixture, and several minutes later it's still sitting there.

This can be caused by a couple of situations. One is that the planting mixture you have is almost completely made of clay. Another is if the planting mixture is old (as with a house-plant that hasn't been changed for years) and it's completely compacted. The last reason is that the root ball has become absolutely choked with roots.

All of these situations are a result of there being no air spaces left for the water to seep downwards through. Either clay soil or compaction or roots are blocking any ability for the water to be pulled down by gravity. To fix this, your job will be to reverse that situation.

The best way is to take the root ball out of the pot and cut away or loosen at least half of the planting mixture. If there are a lot of roots, you'll have to use a sharp knife or garden shears to cut away about a third of them from around the outer edge and bottom of the root ball.

Once you've reduced the size of the root ball, you can re-pot it in the same pot, and fill the spaces with a fresh planting mixture. Make sure it's a mix that drains well and is not too heavy with soil. In Chapter Two there's a recipe for a lightweight container mix that I would recommend, and it's re-printed below.

LIGHTWEIGHT CONTAINER MIX
1 part Potting soil
1 part Compost
2 parts Coir/peat
2 parts Perlite
2 parts Vermiculite

Pest control

As mentioned in my previous book, "*Stuart Robertson's Tips on Organic Gardening*", I would like to propose that you use a more organic approach to pest control.

Healthy well-fed plants will not often need any kind of intervention in the way of pest control, so that's your first line of defense. But if you see a pest problem, don't hesitate to act upon it right away, before it becomes a bigger problem.

The organic approach to pest control usually starts with the least intensive method, such as removal by hand, and only then progresses to using stronger products. Using the term "organic" when related to pesticides has become a metaphor for "harmless to humans" in many peoples' minds. However, it should be pointed out that they're not all harmless. Anything which eventually kills an organism is potentially harmful, and should be treated with respect.

I draw your attention to the fact that *rotenone,* which is derived from botanical sources, has recently been linked to possible causes of Parkinson's disease. Other naturally occurring pesticides can be harmful if ingested or if they come in contact with the eyes or lungs. So be as careful when using "organic" pesticides as you would with any other type.

Organic pesticides are the polar opposite of chemical ones in several respects. They usually target a very specific pest, unlike the broad-spectrum chemical poisons. They usually only work in contact with the pest and don't linger in the environment, as opposed to chemical ones which can stay around in the food chain for a long time. And organics often work because of their physical properties or their specific impact on the pest, rather than their deadliness to all life.

Let me give you some examples. Horticultural oil used as a spray to combat aphids isn't a magic elixir. It simply coats the bodies of insects and eggs to kill them in a purely physical attack. Similarly, diatomaceous earth is composed of minute shards of silica (like glass) that puncture insect bodies and dehydrate them.

However, there are some poisonous organic sprays too. Insecticidal soap affects an amino acid in the stomach of its targets, so they die of hunger. *Bacillus thuringiensis* (Bt) and *bacillus popilliae* are bacteria that kill very specific pests and leave others alone.

In spite of this rather targeted approach to pest control, organics can be harmful to beneficial insects too. Bt can kill butterfly larvae along with the spruce budworm, and rotenone may harm aquatic life. So we still have to be careful when using them not to upset the natural balance of the garden.

Organic pest control

Many organic pesticides come from botanical sources, derived from parts of plants, and were found when gardeners or researchers observed their impact on insects. Others come from mineral, bacterial and viral sources and were deliberately designed or accidentally discovered to affect pests.

Here are some of the more common organic pest controls on the market today. These refer to the generic name or ingredient, as opposed to whatever name the manufacturers have given their versions. Look carefully on the lower section of a pesticide label, usually in very fine print, for the actual active ingredient in the product.

Bacillus thuringiensis (Bt) are bacteria which attacks the stomachs of the larval stage of moths and butterflies. It works on pests such as caterpillar, cutworm, looper, hornworm and budworm. It is usually sold as a concentrate which must be mixed with water and sprayed on contact with the insects. They stop eating and die after a couple of days.

Bacillus popilliae (milky spore disease) are bacteria which attack the larval stage, or grubs, of Japanese beetles and June beetles. A powder or granular mix is dusted on the soil or lawn over the areas affected. Should be applied in the late spring before grubs emerge as adults, and should be done annually in our climate.

Boric acid comes from borax, and is a useful poison against cockroaches and a deterrent of ants. Since it is also toxic to mammals, it should be handled carefully.

Copper has both insecticidal and fungicidal properties, but is most often sold for fungus protection. It is sometimes mixed with lime to increase its effectiveness against fungus. It is most useful dusted or sprayed on foliage to prevent the spread of fungus problems such as leaf spot and powdery mildew. Used either as a powder or in a water spray. Should be applied on susceptible plants **before** the fungus takes hold. Apply with care and avoid contact or breathing dust. Very toxic to fish.

Diatomaceous earth is made from crushed diatoms, which

become sharp shards of silica. These puncture soft insect bodies causing them to dehydrate. May also be mixed with a poison such as rotenone to ensure a faster action. Affected areas must be dusted to contact the insects, and it must be reapplied after rain.

Mineral oil (horticultural oil) makes use of its coating ability to cover and suffocate insects on plants. It is useful against aphid, whitefly and corn worms. A very fine-textured and purified formulation is needed for plant spraying applications.

Neem is named after tree found in India and the southern United States. Since very little research has been done on this product, the reasons for its effects are not well documented. Its taste deters some insects from attacking plants, and can also affect their life cycle. The chemical has not been licensed as an official pesticide in Canada, so it is usually sold as a "leaf cleaner". It works well against aphid, whitefly, moth, leaf miner, thrips and many beetles. Concentrates made from the seeds of the tree are mixed with water and sprayed on the affected foliage.

Pyrethrin is a contact poison extracted from pyrethrum daisies. Since it kills a wide variety of insects and may be toxic to mammals, you should handle it with care. Usually sold as a powder for direct application or mixing with water for a spray.

Rotenone (derris powder) comes from the ground root of a plant, and is a wide spectrum poison which works on beetles. It is toxic to mammals, and can harm fish in ponds, so extreme caution should be taken if using this product.

Soap sprays take advantage of the fact that soapy coatings can smother insects. But research has shown that soaps made from certain fatty acids have insecticidal properties. They attack stomach enzymes and cells of sucking insects such as aphid, whitefly, mealybug and thrips. As a result, several insecticidal soap concentrates are available, to be mixed with water for spraying. The tissue of some plants such as beans and ferns are sensitive to the soap, so test the spray on a small area first. As a result of this, some other soaps have been formulated as herbicides.

Sulphur has both insecticidal and fungicidal properties, which is why it is sometimes sold as a combined fungus and insect treatment. It is sometimes mixed with lime to increase its effectiveness against fungus. It is most useful dusted or sprayed on foliage to prevent the spread of fungus problems such as leaf spot and powdery mildew. Used either as a powder or in a water spray. Should be applied on susceptible plants **before** the fungus takes hold. Apply with care and avoid contact or breathing dust.

Home-made pesticides

There are several home-made versions of pesticide sprays which you can try before resorting to more poisonous ones. Soap is often added to make the spray cling to leaf surfaces. Here are a few recipes.

Baking soda fungicide for precautionary use against black spot and mildew. Mix one tablespoon of baking soda in one litre of water and shake well. Warm water helps it to dissolve faster. Then add one teaspoon of liquid dish soap. Spray all surfaces of problem plants **before** the fungus takes hold.

Garlic spray concentrate which can work against aphid, whitefly, cabbage and tomato worms. Put three crushed garlic cloves into enough mineral oil to cover them, and soak overnight. Then in a separate container put one teaspoon of liquid dish soap into half a litre of water. Mix the garlic-soaked mineral oil in with the soapy water, and store in a sealed container. When you want to spray, add two tablespoons of the garlic spray concentrate with half a litre of water and spray all surfaces of the foliage.

General-purpose bug spray which can be effective against chewing and sucking insects such as aphid, chafer, whitefly and thrips. Blend one whole garlic, one small onion and a tablespoon of cayenne pepper in a food processor. Add to one litre of water and mix well. Let stand for one hour. Strain the mixture through a fine sieve or cheesecloth. Add one tablespoon of liquid dish soap. Spray all surfaces of affected plants every two days. Store refrigerated for up to a week.

Most common insect pests

Pest: Aphid (many varieties), a.k.a. plant lice.

Hosts: Young tips of plants (flowers, vegetables, and shrubs).

Damage: Adults suck juice from leaves and stems, causing mottled markings, secrete liquid "honeydew" which attracts ants and fungus. Can transmit disease between plants.

Controls: For eggs: Wipe leaf and stem surfaces with a soapy cloth to remove eggs. Spray with horticultural oil in early spring to smother eggs (best used on shrubs).

For adults: Spray with water to dislodge. Use yellow sticky paper to attract and trap. Spray with insecticidal soap or neem. Dust with diatomaceous earth.

Pest: Ant

Host: Not often found on plants.

Damage: Ants are not pests. They seldom cause damage to plants. On occasion they may collect and protect aphids to eat the "honeydew" excreted by the aphids.

Controls: If you control the aphids (see above) the ants will move on. Ants are very useful predators in the garden, and should not be attacked. If ants become a nuisance indoors, they can be discouraged with borax in crystal or spray format.

Pest: Beetle (various types).

Hosts: Mostly prey on other insects, a few plants.

Damage: Seldom do serious damage to plants, but might discolour some leaves. Mainly feed on eggs and larvae of other insects.

Controls: Not often needed. Flea Beetles can be controlled with diatomaceous earth, rotenone or neem. Japanese Beetles and June Beetles are best controlled when they do damage underground in their larval stage (grubs) with milky spore disease (*bacillus popilliae*) or nematode treatment. Must be applied in late spring/early summer while grubs active.

Pest: Borer (larval stage of several insects).
Hosts: Trees, vegetable crops.
Damage: Bore into and enter plant stems, causing wilting.
Controls: Watch for evidence of wilting. Look for the entrance hole in the stem near the ground, slit open the stem just above the hole and kill the borer. Cover the wounded stem with soil.

Pest: Caterpillar, looper, hornworm, budworm (larval stage of butterflies and moths).
Hosts: Trees, shrubs, vegetables.
Damage: Eat whole sections of foliage, fruit.
Controls: Physical removal of nests (dispose of by burning or drowning). Spray target foliage with garlic/onion/pepper mix to discourage being eaten. Spray larvae with Bt (*bacillus thuringiensis*) or neem.

Pest: Cutworm (larval stage of moth).
Hosts: Young flower and vegetable seedlings.
Damage: Chew on and cut stems of seedlings just below the surface.
Controls: Place foil or plastic collar around seedlings at planting time, extending two inches underground, to protect the stems. Mix moist bran with Bt and spread on the surface a week before planting.

Pest: Earwig.
Hosts: Decorative and vegetable plants.

Damage: Minor foliage damage from young. Adults scavenge through garden debris.

Controls: Not often needed. Can be deterred with diatomaceous earth.

Pest: Leafhopper, spittlebug.

Hosts: Garden plants.

Damage: Small numbers of insects cause very little damage. Can sometimes transmit disease causing stunting, discoloured leaves.

Controls: Spray with water to remove. Dust with diatomaceous earth for major infestations.

Pest: Leaf miner (larval stage of fly).

Hosts: Some trees and decorative plants.

Damage: Larvae tunnel between tissues of leaves, causing pale tracks.

Controls: Remove affected leaves and destroy. For trees, place a sticky band around the trunk in spring to trap the crawling stage. Spray with neem.

Pest: Lily beetle (like a lady beetle but without spots).

Hosts: Lily stems and leaves.

Damage: Slug-like larvae eat the foliage, adults eat the foliage. Plants can be stripped in a few days.

Controls: All stages must be attacked as soon as possible to stop the breeding cycle.

For eggs: Surrounded with black slime, should be wiped off with a soapy cloth.

For larvae: Remove with water spray. Dust with diatomaceous earth or rotenone.

For adults: Physical removal (destroy or drop into soapy water). Spray with neem. Dust with diatomaceous earth or rotenone.

Pest: Slug.
Hosts: Ornamental plant foliage.
Damage: Chew holes in foliage at night, leaving slime trails.
Controls: They prefer smooth damp surfaces, so surrounding plants with dry wood ash or grit can slow their passage. Stale beer in saucers will attract them to drown. Salt burns them if applied directly. Copper mesh or strips will deter them. Granules of iron sulphate and bait (sold commercially) placed in covered traps will attract and kill them, and last through rainfalls.

Pest: Thrips (always referred to in the plural).
Hosts: Flowers and foliage of ornamentals, vegetables.
Damage: Scrape plant skin and suck sap. Nymphs and adults cause streaks and blemishes on flowers, twisting and distortion of leaves.
Controls: Spray with insecticidal soap or neem. Dust with diatomaceous earth or rotenone.

Pest: Whitefly.
Hosts: Flowers and vegetables.
Damage: Adults suck juice from leaves and flowers, causing spotted appearance.
Controls: For eggs: wipe underside of leaves with a soapy cloth to remove.

For adults: Cover any infested plants with large plastic bag to trap and prevent adult flies from moving to other plants, and then spray with insecticidal soap or neem.

Most common fungus problems
The most effective way to avoid fungus infestations is to avoid the conditions that encourage them. It's not possible to control the damp weather, but you can avoid spraying plant foliage with water unnecessarily, and you can avoid crowding your plants which in turn reduces air circulation.

It also helps to catch fungus attacks as soon as they start and never let them go any further. This means quickly cleaning up and destroying diseased foliage as well as using fungus control products.

Growing disease-resistant varieties also helps, as does spreading mulch to reduce the spread of fungus spores from soil to foliage.

Pest: Downy and powdery mildew, black spot, leaf spot (all forms of fungus disease).

Host: Various ornamentals, vegetables. Most active during periods of wet weather, both cool and warm.

Damage: Gradually harms plant tissue. Leaves fall, fruit and flowers can be affected. Spreads quickly once established.

Controls: For prevention, avoid spraying water on foliage, keep plants un-crowded, and pruned to be open to air circulation. For treatment, use sulphur-based and copper-based spray, or for mild infestations a mix of baking soda in water may suffice.

Pest: Wilt disease (resulting from fungus). Most common varieties are verticillium (V) and fusarium (F).

Host: Tomato family (non-resistant varieties).

Damage: Blockage of water-conducting tissue causes parts of the plant to die. Usually starts with lower leaves which shrivel and die, and gradually works upwards through the whole plant. Fruit may be able to ripen in spite of this.

Controls: No direct controls possible. Remove any affected foliage and destroy. Plant in different locations on a three year cycle. Plant wilt-resistant varieties (shown as "V, F resistant").

Most common animal pests

We share our environment with the animals which inhabit it, from the deer and groundhogs in rural areas to the raccoons and squirrels that live in our cities. Sometimes they become pests, using our gardens as a food supply. But remember, they're just doing what comes naturally to them.

If it becomes necessary to deter and discourage these visitors, it should be done humanely. However, it will require a lot of cunning because these four-legged pests are intelligent and persistent. There are no magic potions or fool-proof methods for keeping them out of the garden. Often it's a matter of trying several methods one after the other as their effect wears off, or trying a whole bunch at once.

However, after suffering from the ravages of deer in a country garden for years, all I can say is "good luck" and keep trying.

Pest: Deer.

Host: Anything which attracts them. Anything.

Damage: From nibbling of tips to complete destruction.

Controls: A series of different methods done one after the other seems to be the best approach. As they get used to one after a couple of weeks, you switch to another. Here are some of the recommended methods. They run from the least expensive (and least effective) to the most expensive (and most effective). Hang pie plates or CD's to twist in the wind. String fishing line around the protected area, about three feet off the ground. Wrap kerosene-soaked cloth around sticks and place the sticks around the garden. Hang up bars of Irish Spring soap (because they don't like it too!). Hang up bunches of human hair. Spray patches with the urine of dogs, wolves, mountain lions or tigers (I'm not saying this is easy, just that it's been reported to work!). Water sprayers controlled by motion sensors. Deer repellants made with foul-smelling mixtures, to be daubed on plants or on sticks. Fences, either eight feet high (if vertical), or six-strands spread over ten feet and placed at a 45 degree angle. Two parallel four-foot high fences placed six feet apart. Dog patrols between the fences. Live mountain lions and tigers roaming your garden. You get the idea.

Pest: Domestic cats and dogs.

Host: Lawns and tall plants.

Damage: Urine spray which can kill foliage.

Controls: Once the urine spraying starts, the smell will attract them even more. Wash affected plants with a hose. Dilute urine on lawns as soon as possible after it's done. A low fence, even a foot high, is usually enough to deter a passing dog (**and its owner**) from going onto a lawn. There are spray products which use scents to discourage a return to the same place. Water sprayers controlled by motion sensors also work for cats, and they learn quickly not to come back. Lion and tiger patrols.

Pest: Raccoons.

Host: Perfectly ripe fruit (they know the exact moment), insects and grubs in the lawn.

Damage: From small bites to complete loss.

Controls: Not much can deter this curious and nimble predator. Physical barriers such as netting can be set up to protect tomato plants, but protecting rows of corn, berries or grape vines is a major problem. They are not scared of cats, but a dog will keep them away. However, they are most active at night when barking dogs are least appreciated by neighbours. You could try the motion-sensor controlled water spray. Perhaps the foul-smelling deer repellants would keep them away.

Pest: Squirrels.

Host: Some fruit.

Damage: Bitten fruit and flowers, holes dug in gardens and containers for some purpose known only to the squirrel.

Controls: Physical barriers such as netting over fruit can slow them down. In spring they cut the heads off tulip blooms, and I'm told they are looking to drink the water from the cut stem and not to eat the petals. Put out small bowls of sugar water instead. Dust tulips with a mix of cayenne pepper and chili powder (does not work on squirrels from the Tex-Mex regions!). By the way, I have it on good authority that this mix does **not** cause the squirrels to scratch their eyes out. The water-spraying motion-sensor triggered device will deter them. Dogs and cats also deter squirrels a little, but then I have to re-refer you to "Domestic cats and dogs" above.

Cleaning containers
Keeping your containers clean is more than just a matter of neatness. Although being tidy is an aspect you should be considering, cleanliness is also a way of fighting pests.

When you put away a dirty container at the end of one season and keep it until the next, you are potentially carrying over insect eggs, fungus spores and viruses. So it pays to keep things clean.

My advice would be to put away your containers clean in the autumn, rather that facing it as yet another task in the spring. You'll start fresh, and there won't be any temptation to "put it off till next year".

There are a few different things that may need cleaning off your containers, and each of them needs a slightly different approach.

Dirt. The easiest way to clean the dirt off the inside and outside of containers is with water and a stiff brush. Along with the dirt you may be removing bits of root fibre and plant material, so I'd suggest doing it outdoors so that these bits and pieces don't end up going down your drain to potentially clog it.

Calcium. If your water is high in calcium content, you may also see deposits of white powder on your container. If it's a porous one, such as terra cotta, the deposits will be on the outside of the container where it leached through. If it's a non-porous container, you may see a crust of white calcium around the edges at the top of the planting mixture.

This calcium will dissolve in a mixture of one part vinegar to three parts water. Mix up a small batch and scrub the deposits off with a stiff brush. In the case of terra cotta pots, you may have to soak them in this mixture for an hour to dissolve the calcium that's just beneath the clay surface.

Algae. Containers can also become covered in a green-coloured deposit. These are the remains of algae that grew on the surface of the container. They grew there as a result of having perfect conditions, with a good supply of nutrients, warmth, moisture and of course some algae cells to get the whole thing going.

The algae growth is not serious, and can be removed with a mild bleach solution in water.

However, with some terra cotta or stone containers the growth of algae or moss on the surface can give them an aged look which people find attractive. If you actually want to get that look as quickly as possible on your container, there's a trick for getting the growth established on even a brand new container.

Take a small handful of moss (from a rock or tree) and crumble it up into a blender. Add a cup or two of milk or buttermilk. Blend the mixture until it's reasonably consistent, and then spread the glop over portions of the container that you want to "age". Very soon, the moss will produce a film of green growth wherever it was spread, and you'll have an ancient looking container in no time.

If you have any other container-related problems, you can contact me at stuartrobertsontips@gmail.com

Glossary

Annual A plant that grows from seed to maturity in one season.

Biennial A plant that flowers and seeds in the second season from seed germination.

Dead-heading Removing flowers that have finished blooming. If left on the plant, they will set seeds and thereby slow the growth of the plant.

Coir This is a natural product, made from the fibres of the outer husk of a coconut. The fibres absorb several times their weight in water, and take a long time to break down. It is a substitute for peat.

Compost The material that results from the decomposition of various animal, vegetable and mineral materials. It is a source of fibre, humus and fertilizer and is used as a soil additive.

Fertilizing Adding selected nutrients to the soil which will dissolve and provide plants with food. The main elements are; nitrogen (N) for stem and leaf growth, phosphor (P) to develop strong root systems as well as flower and fruit growth, and potassium (K) which is mainly responsible for tissue strength, disease resistance and fruit development. The ratio of NPK is always listed on a fertilizer package, e.g. 5-10-5. Carbon, hydrogen and oxygen are essential too, but are available from the air. Other nutrients needed in small quantities are calcium and magnesium. Only trace amounts of boron, chlorine, copper, iron, manganese, molybdenum, sulphur and zinc are needed.

Foliar feeding Spraying a weak solution of liquid fertilizer on the foliage of a plant. Best done mid-season on large plants to assist growth. A recommended use for dilute "manure tea", made by soaking a sack of manure in a bucket of water overnight. Foliar feeding should be done in conjunction with feeding the soil (see **Fertilizing**).

Germination When a seed starts to grow and splits open to produce a root and a stem.

Heading back Pruning the tips of shrub and tree branches to stop further growth. This will result in a more dense growth of side shoots and foliage at the outer edges of the plant (see **Thinning**).

Hardening-off Toughening up plants (usually seedlings) which which have been grown under cover, so that they can be planted outdoors with no risk of shock. Consists of gradual exposure to sun, wind, rain and outdoor temperature flucuations.

Hydroponic containers These are self-watering containers that are filled with a soiless medium and control the feeding of plants by using a nutrient solution in place of plain water.

Mulching Covering exposed soil with a blanket of some other material. This stops moisture evaporating from the soil, and chokes weed germination and growth. Common mulches are shredded wood, bark chips, grass clippings, cocoa bean hulls, straw, plastic film, spun fibre sheets, shredded newspaper. It reduces the need for weeding and watering (see **Cultivating**).

Node The point on a plant stem from where a leaf or stem will grow. The sections between nodes are inter-nodes.

Perennial A plant that lasts through many seasons.

Perlite This is a man-made product, made from volcanic rock that's been heated to create rough lightweight white granules about the size of lentils. Because of its rough texture it holds some moisture on its surface while absorbing very little. It is relatively inert and provides no nutrients. In a planting mixture it encourages good drainage, and its lighter weight often makes it more advantageous than sand.

Pinching Cutting off the growing tip of a stem, often done with the thumbnail and forefinger. Similar to **Heading**. This slows tip growth and forces new growth to sprout from behind the cut, resulting in denser, more compact growth. Useful on annuals and perennials to encourage more flower heads.

Planter A container that is usually large enough to make it difficult to move once filled with planting mixture.

Planting mixture The medium that plants are planted into in containers. It is not usually pure soil, but rather a mixture of various products that provide a suitable home for the plants, and these components can be adjusted to make a variety of mixtures with differing properties.

Root pruning Trimming a quantity of the roots off a plant. Normally done to encourage new root growth in container-ized plants, or to prepare a large soil-bound plant to be moved. When pruning off roots, a similar quantity of foliage should be removed to avoid stress to the plant.

Shrub A plant with many woody stems growing out of the ground, rather than one single stem.

Soiless mixtures These are planting mixtures blended without any soil or compost ingredients. They are made from products such as peat, perlite and vermiculite, or they use porous clay pellets, gravel or rock wool. The soiless products absorb moisture and hold plant roots. Since they contain no nutrients at all, it is necessary to feed the plants with a nutrient solution.

Summer bulbs These are a collection of tender bulbs, tubers, corms and rhizomes that are not hardy enough to withstand freezing temperatures (see **Tender**), and therefore must be lifted from the planting mixture and stored indoors for the winter.

Tender When used in describing plants (e.g. tender bulbs or tender shrubs) it refers to the fact that they are not hardy enough to withstand below-freezing temperatures. This means they have to be grown or stored indoors whenever the temperatures are below freezing.

Terra cotta A material made from kiln-fired clay frequently used in garden pots. Unglazed it is slightly porous. Glazing inside or out makes it waterproof.

Thinning Pruning out whole branches from a shrub or tree, to relieve congested growth. Usually the oldest branches are removed first. This results in a more open structure and stronger growth of the remaining branches. (see **Heading**)

Top dressing Spreading fertilizer on the surface around a plant, without disturbing the plant roots, so that watering and rain will wash it into the soil. Use slow-release granular fertilizer, liquid fertilizer or compost. Side dressing is doing the same, but on either side of a row of plants.

Transplanting Moving a plant or section of a plant into a new location. Care must be taken to prepare the new planting hole with a suitable soil mix and moisture supply to encourage new root growth. Transplanting is best done in early spring or late fall when plants are less active and temperature stress is lower.

Vermiculite This is a man-made product, made from mica that's been heated until it expands to form lightweight granules. Because of its sponge-like construction, it holds several times its weight in water, as well as some air. It is quite inert and provides no nutrient value.

Window box A container that is usually hung or supported below a window or along a railing. It is usually long and narrow in dimensions, but should be as deep as possible.

References

Biles, R.E.: "The Complete Book of Gardening Magic",
J.G.Ferguson, Illinois, 1946.

Borrer, D.J., and DeLong, D.M.: "An Introduction to the
Study of Insects", Saunders College Publishing, Texas, 1989.

Christopher, E.P.: "Introductory Horticulture", McGraw-
Hill Book Company Inc., New York, 1958.

Cranshaw, W.: "Garden Insects of North America", Prince-
ton University Press, New Jersey, 2004.

Cutting, A.B.: "Canadian Home Gardening" Second Edition,
The Musson Book Company, Ontario, 1951.

Drysdale, A.C.: "Gardening Off the Ground", J.M.Dent &
Sons Canada Ltd., Toronto, 1975.

Ellis, B.W., and Bradley, F.M.: "Natural Insect and Disease
Control", Rodale Press, Pennsylvania, 1992.

Gustafson, A.F.: "Using and Managing Soils", McGraw-Hill
Book Company Inc., New York, 1948.

Purnell, R.: "Crops in Pots", Octopus Publishing, London,
2007.

Thompson, L.M.: "Soils and Soil Fertility", McGraw-Hill
Book Company Inc., New York, 1952.

Vick, E.C., "Audels Gardeners and Growers Guide", Audel
& Co., New York, 1928.

Westcott, C.: "The Gardener's Bug Book", Fourth Edition,
Doubleday & Company, New York, 1972.

Index

[Notes]

[Notes]

[Notes]

Véhicule Press

www.vehiculepress.com